Developing interactive teaching and learning using the IWB

A resource for teachers

Developing interactive teaching and learning using the IWB

A resource for teachers

Sara Hennessy, Paul Warwick, Lloyd Brown, Diane Rawlins and Caroline Neale

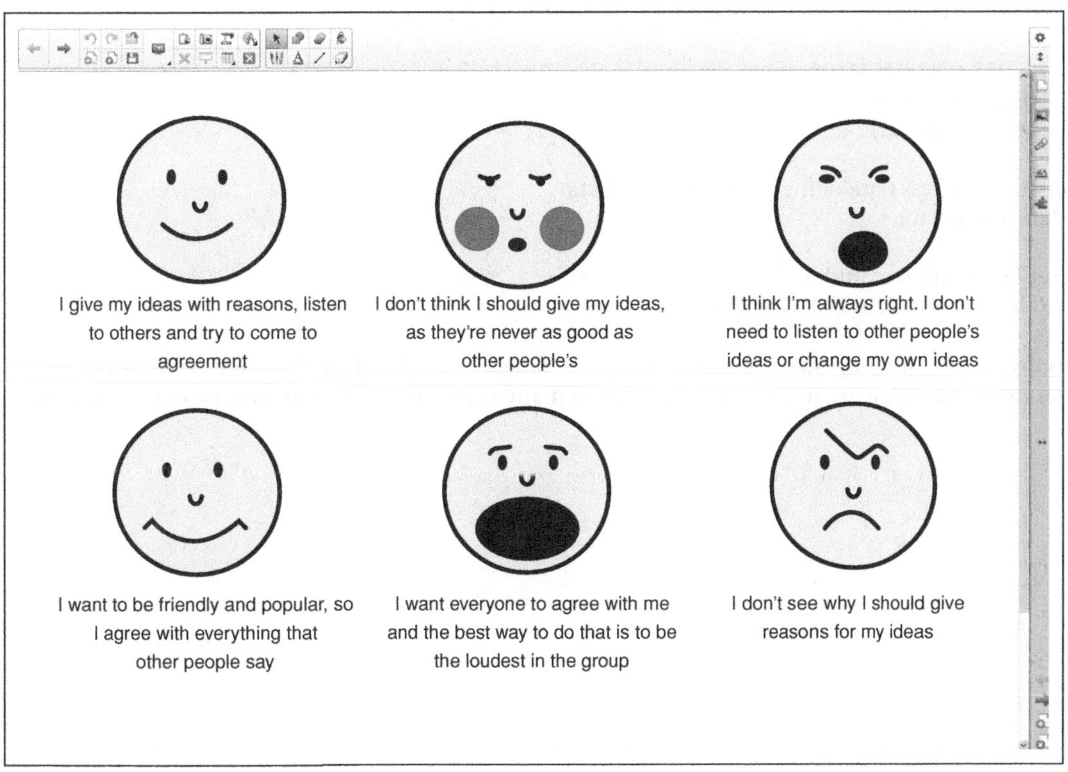

Mc Graw Hill Education Open University Press

Open University Press
McGraw-Hill Education
McGraw-Hill House
Shoppenhangers Road
Maidenhead
Berkshire
England
SL6 2QL

email: enquiries@openup.co.uk
world wide web: www.openup.co.uk

and Two Penn Plaza, New York, NY 10121-2289, USA

First published 2014

A catalogue record of this book is available from the British Library

ISBN-13: 978-0-335-26316-5
ISBN-10: 0-335-26316-X
eISBN: 978-0-335-26317-2

Library of Congress Cataloging-in-Publication Data
CIP data applied for

Typeset by Aptara Inc., India
Printed by Bell and Bain Ltd, Glasgow

Praise for this book

"This valuable resource provides both a theoretical framework and pedagogic guidance on how to use the interactive whiteboard to its full potential with learners of all ages. Written by established classroom practitioners and academic researchers, it provides a set of resources which are grounded in the reality of classroom life, but underpinned by academic rigour which make it useful to both student and experienced teachers alike."

Professor Gary Beauchamp, Professor of Education and Director of Research, School of Education, Cardiff Metropolitan University, UK

"I fully recommend this set of extremely useful materials containing a strong classroom voice endorsed by authoritative academic researchers. Teachers will be drawn to this material, and will be able to review their own practice, reflect on the centrality of classroom spoken interactions, and investigate how best to use the expensive item of technology on the wall to get the very best from their investment. The blend of resources, ideas and readings coupled with the video clips will provide a wealth of material to do just that.

It will prove very useful for teachers with any length of experience, from those who might want to take a fresh look at their classroom practice to those new to the profession. I will certainly draw from this in my CPD training with school staff."

Sally Elding, Senior Adviser, Primary Elearning Team, The ICT Service, Cambridgeshire

"This book ensures that 'interactivity' in the classroom does not just mean the casual interaction of students with software. Instead, the authors show how to combine two very powerful tools – the IWB and talk – to create an effective and inclusive learning environment. Chapters draw on classroom settings to show how use of the IWB can be enhanced by a focus on the quality of the talk that goes on between students, and between teacher and learners. Authors use practical experience to highlight the things that make the difference to the use of the IWB – for example the establishment of exploratory dialogue, the thoughtful organisation of group work and the creation of straightforward but stimulating IWB resources. In addition the text provides clear guidance for teachers on how and why to raise student awareness of the importance of their discussion when making or considering digital artefacts. There is a strong focus on ensuring that both students and teachers understand best use of the IWB; and that contexts for learning are provided which really merit discussion.

The Teacher Development section considers use of the IWB in a dialogic classroom – and shows how best practice can be achieved, with useful resources, and a format for reviewing own learning.

The Reader section provides insight into the aspects of talk that fit together to generate a dialogic classroom context, and crucially shows how use of the IWB is both enhanced by dialogue and contributes to students' capacity to take part in learning dialogues with one another.

The Resource Bank draws on a range of classroom contexts, providing examples to support teachers as they create their own lesson plans and ideas.

The text is accessible and interesting, with complex ideas clearly explained, and the book is readily navigated.

This book will enable teachers to plan for dialogue based on the motivating and interesting features of the IWB. In particular it provides guidance for student use of the IWB, and creation of own resources tailored to learning needs. Teachers who wish to have a focus on dialogue will find here a theoretically based, practical approach to ensuring that their students really benefit from interactivity, with the IWB and with each other."

Dr Lyn Dawes, Educational Consultant

Contents

APPENDICES

Contributors

The main resource was co-authored by two university researchers and three experienced, practising teachers who previously collaborated on a research project to develop and analyse classroom practice using the interactive whiteboard (IWB) to support dialogue. Two further colleagues, Simon Knight and Rupert Wegerif, kindly contributed chapters to the Reader section, and Neil Mercer wrote the Foreword.

Lloyd Brown is a history teacher and Deputy Head at Chesterton Community College in Cambridge. With 24 years' experience, he has taught subjects including History, RE, Leisure and Tourism, PE, Business Studies and Geography. At Chesterton, Lloyd works with PGCE and Graduate Teacher Programme trainees as Professional Tutor, leads in-service training in school and has previously participated in research within the Cambridge University-schools partnership (SUPER), most recently concentrating on dialogic teaching. In the past he held three Department for Education and Science (DfES)-funded Best Practice Research Scholarships investigating 'multisource learning', development of oracy, and intra- and interpersonal multiple intelligences.

Sara Hennessy is a Senior Lecturer in Teacher Development and Pedagogical Innovation in the Faculty of Education at the University of Cambridge. She has over two decades of experience of research into subject teaching and learning using technology, including supporting professional development in using information and communication technology (ICT) in subject teaching. She has carried out a number of studies of IWB use in classrooms and most recently explored the potential of the tool to support classroom learning through dialogue. Her work also focuses on understanding and developing pedagogy, practitioner–researcher partnerships and collaborative theory building, and ICT use in sub-Saharan African schools including creating professional learning resources for interactive primary mathematics and science teaching – with and without ICT – in Zambia.

Simon Knight is a Teaching Associate in the University of Cambridge's Faculty of Education, and a Doctor of Philosophy (PhD) student in the Open University's Knowledge Media Institute. He completed his PGCE in Social Sciences and Master's in the Philosophy of Education at the Institute of Education, London. Following teaching (mostly Advanced level philosophy and psychology) in a school south of Cambridge he returned to academia. His research focuses on the implications of technologies – particularly search engines – for how individuals manage information, how educators assess knowledge and, more broadly, how we conceptualize knowledge and understanding. He is particularly interested in applying a sociocultural and philosophical approach to these issues and tweets about his research @sjgknight.

Neil Mercer (the author of our Foreword) is Professor of Education at the University of Cambridge. He is a psychologist with a special interest in classroom dialogue and the development of children's thinking, who has also led several projects on science and mathematics education and the use of ICT in schools. Neil has been a consultant to the government's department of education and curriculum authority (in their various incarnations) and local authorities throughout the UK. His most recent books are *Words and Minds: How We Use Language to Think Together, Dialogue and the Development of Children's Thinking* (with Karen Littleton) and *Exploring Talk in School* (with Steve Hodgkinson).

Caroline Neale is an English and drama teacher at King's College School, Cambridge. With 11 years' experience, she previously worked as Head of English and Drama at Greneway Middle School in Royston, where she started to develop her interest in using both the IWB and dialogue as tools for learning. Her participation in the IWB and Dialogue research project then led to the completion of a Master of Education in Leading Teaching and Learning at Cambridge University, where her focus was on how a dialogic approach to teaching and learning could be successfully implemented at a whole-school level.

Diane Rawlins is Deputy Headteacher of Arbury Primary School, a large, urban primary school in Cambridge. She has been teaching at primary schools for 16 years, mostly with 10- to 11-year-olds, but is now out of class full time. She is specifically responsible in school for pupil voice, pastoral care, curriculum development, developing the quality of teaching and learning, and mentoring trainee and newly qualified teachers. Diane has been involved in a number of small-scale research projects over recent years and is especially interested in exploring how we can develop dialogic teaching approaches within our school setting. She is at present studying part-time for her Master of Education (MEd) in Critical Approaches to Children's Literature at Cambridge University Faculty of Education.

Paul Warwick is a Lecturer in Primary Science and ICT in the Faculty of Education at the University of Cambridge. He is engaged in a range of research and teaching activities in the faculty that link directly with his interests in primary science education, the uses of ICT in teaching and learning, and the professional development of trainee and beginning teachers. His work on the classroom uses of the IWB has focused on children's active involvement in the use of the IWB for collaborative group learning and on teachers' uses of the IWB in the context of a dialogic pedagogy. Paul is a member of the Early Years and Primary Masters Postgraduate Certificate of Education (PGCE) team. His involvement in teacher education has taken him to various countries in Africa and Europe, and to the USA. He is a member of the editorial board of the journal *Reflective Teaching*.

Rupert Wegerif is Professor of Education at the University of Exeter. He has researched and published widely on dialogic approaches to education usually with technology and sometimes in relation to teaching thinking. He is currently working on several projects investigating (1) talk in classrooms, (2) tools to support computer supported collaborative learning and (3) dialogue across cultural differences in science education. He is co-editor of *Thinking Skills and Creativity*, an international journal with Elsevier. His latest books are: *Mindexpanding: Teaching for Thinking and Creativity*, which offers some practical approaches, and *Dialogic: Education for the Internet Age*, which explains the new kind of education we need for the future.

Foreword

Neil Mercer

The eminent educational researcher Douglas Barnes, a former English teacher, once said that classroom education floats on a sea of talk. Talk is the main tool of a teacher's trade, and it plays a key role in mediating children's educational experience. Much attention has been given to analysing and understanding its functions in recent years, but the ephemeral and everyday nature of talk tends still to make it a taken-for-granted feature of life in school. Yet we know that by improving the quality of dialogue in classrooms, we can improve the quality of students' participation, learning and their levels of attainment. The material included in this collection draws on recent studies of classroom dialogue, and especially on those that offer useful insights and practical guidance for teachers.

Today, digital technology has also become, for a great many teachers and students, another taken-for-granted, background feature of life in school (and in the rest of life too, of course). But like any expensive tool, digital technology needs to be employed effectively to justify its use. Interactive whiteboards are fast becoming a standard feature of the classroom in many parts of the world. As the material in this collection shows, they can be very useful tools for teachers wishing to enhance the quality of dialogue in their classrooms. Included here is some very useful practical guidance for planning and employing such educational technology in everyday school environments. Overall, this collection brings together a unique set of resources that should be valuable for teachers and educators working in a range of professional situations.

Acknowledgements

The IWBs and Dialogue research study was funded mainly by the UK Economic and Social Research Council (ref. RES-063-27-0081) and partly by a small grant from the Isaac Newton Trust at University of Cambridge.

Thanks are extended to the four peer reviewers for their supportive and informative comments on the resource proposal.

We are very grateful, too, to Laura Flitton for her rigorous pilot trials of the draft resource in schools, and to all of the teachers who participated in our workshops and evaluation activities, and/or contributed their ideas and materials to the Resource Bank. In particular, Laura Flitton, Andrew Cornick and Chris Tooley prepared the SMART Notebook and ActivInspire template files for us. All IWB screenshots and materials in this resource were devised by teachers, and are reproduced here with their kind permission.

Simon Knight assisted with preparation of some Reader chapters and with their integration into the resource. Neil Mercer contributed to the design and analysis of the underlying research and to the team workshop material. His work with Lyn Dawes and Rupert Wegerif on 'Thinking Together' provided much inspiration.

Fiona Richman, Hannah Girt and Sarah Fleming of Open University Press provided helpful assistance in producing this resource. We also thank Lucian Stephenson for his creative design of the graphic overview.

Guided Tour

This resource offers a structured approach to developing your practice in using the IWB, with a particular focus on interactive teaching and learning.

The resource has the following component parts:

- Teacher Development Resource
- Reader containing seven chapters
- Resource Bank (with ideas and IWB templates that you can trial)
- Appendices including teacher resources
- Further online resources (http://tinyurl.com/OUPIWB)

The book, containing the Teacher Development Resource, Reader and Resource Bank, is intended to be used alongside the supporting materials and video clips contained in the appendices or online. Together these can be used as a basis for discussion, reflection and trialling of new ideas.

A significant section of the resource is given over to a Reader, featuring the writings of teachers and academics who have engaged with these ideas through research and classroom practice. The Teacher Development Resource directs you to read each chapter at pertinent points.

The online resources which accompany this book are a useful addition for anyone reading the book, as well as for anyone who wants to provide staff development for interactive teaching and learning with the IWB. They include the video clips that support the activities in the Teacher Development section, demonstrating the more interactive approaches in practice.

The online Resource Bank includes the same Dialogue and IWB activity descriptions with screen-shots that are printed in Part C of this resource; in the online version you can search for specific resources and view screenshots in colour.

The online resources also include IWB templates to help get you started in trialling some of the ideas covered in the resource.

Within the Teacher Development section icons are used throughout the text to help guide you through the resource as explained below:

Table A01

	Refer to item in the appendix
	Read the relevant chapter from the Reader section
	View a video clip online
	Reflection
	Denotes the start of an activity
	Denotes individual tasks within an activity
	Weblink
	Links to content online

The Teacher Development Resource contains:

- coverage of the notions of dialogue and dialogic teaching and the role of the IWB
- the 'dialogue tables' which concisely summarize what happens in a dialogic classroom and what dialogic activity could lead to
- 'snippets', or excerpts, from the research literature and from the Reader chapters
- an action plan document for a whole school approach to setting up and reviewing practice via staff meetings; this resource for senior managers of schools can be adapted for use by smaller groups or with other schools.

The Reader includes:

- seven Reader chapters containing concise background readings, that report in an accessible way on the research underpinning this resource and offering more in-depth illustrations from authentic classroom practice, along with reflections upon them
- references for further reading.

The Resource Bank offers:

- sample and template IWB activities
- a large bank of video clips and screenshots illustrating whole-class dialogue and dialogue in small groups in action plus brief descriptions of the classroom activities
- lesson flipcharts associated with the Reader case study Chapters 2–4.

PART A

The teacher development resource

Developing interactive teaching and learning using the IWB

1 Introduction and use of the resource

1.1 What is this resource for?

This volume provides a professional development resource for teachers who want to develop a more interactive approach to teaching and learning in their classrooms, in particular by engaging students in dialogue, and who are interested in the use of the interactive whiteboard (IWB) as a powerful tool for supporting this approach. There is an increasing number of resources becoming available to support classroom dialogue as a tool for learning, as interest in the approach grows, but this is the first, comprehensive professional learning resource that focuses on using the IWB in that context. Using the resource will help you generate new insights and strategies for developing classroom practice.

The resource offers structured approaches to development, together with supporting materials and web-based video clips that can be used as a *stimulus* for discussion, reflection and trialling of new ideas. A significant section of the resource is given over to a Reader, featuring the writings of teachers and academics who have engaged with these ideas through research and classroom practice. The resource as a whole should not, therefore, be seen as a model to copy; rather, it is a flexible set of materials and resources that can be used as appropriate to your specific professional circumstances.

The aims of this resource are to:

- guide you in building on what you do now by trying out some new ideas for using the IWB in your classroom, either individually or in collaboration with colleagues
- offer a tool for analysing classroom interaction, with a particular focus on how using the IWB with a dialogic intention in mind could help you to improve the quality of teaching and learning in your classroom.

The materials are usable at primary or secondary levels, and across subject areas. They encourage you to take up opportunities to make your practice as 'dialogic' as possible, using the IWB as an aid, but do not ask you to fundamentally rework your approach; effective teaching contains a wide repertoire of different strategies that are used appropriately and dialogic interaction is only one of those (Mortimer and Scott 2003; Alexander 2008). However, what we hope these materials will help you consider is the value of making your classroom *more* of a 'dialogic space' for learning, using the tools at your disposal – in this case, the IWB – to create a supportive ethos for dialogue. This includes taking every opportunity to engage students in a variety of carefully planned forms of dialogic interaction and activity, both away from and at the board, and it includes active participation in extended tasks at the board, in addition to reflection on teacher-focused IWB tasks or projected resources.

While most of the examples offered in the resource are from whole-class teaching, individual and small-group work are equally important in supporting dialogue; we thus include a Reader chapter about group work with the IWB and some related examples of practice in this area.

1.2 How might the resource be used?

As we have suggested above, it is useful to think of this resource as a guided programme of action research and development that can either be followed in a structured manner or dipped into and out of as you wish. It can be used:

- in face-to-face sessions with colleagues
- as a stimulus for colleagues working across school, perhaps via a virtual learning environment
- by individuals working through the materials at home, or
- through a combination of these modes.

The programme might be self-led by participants, for example during a series of staff meetings, or led by an external facilitator.

It is thus suitable for many different professional audiences, including:

1. individuals working alone (entirely, or returning at strategic points for discussions with colleagues)
2. colleagues working together via a virtual learning environment

3. pairs/small groups within a subject department or school year group (perhaps later joining up with other pairs/groups)
4. whole-subject department or whole-school staff body
5. advisers, consultants, advanced skills teachers, professional development leaders, mentors or teacher educators working with groups of pre-service or in-service teachers or teaching assistants who want to develop more dialogic approaches.

1.3 What kinds of activities are involved?

The resource includes stimuli for:

- understanding what dialogue is and how it differs from classroom talk
- reading about and seeing concrete examples of dialogue in action
- auditing your own teaching in terms of supporting dialogue
- seeing what role the IWB can play in supporting whole-class dialogue and dialogue in small groups
- thinking about and discussing how useful/feasible these ideas might be in your setting
- trying out a new idea in class and having a colleague observe you
- looking at teacher strategies for supporting dialogue with the IWB
- reflecting on your own strategies (on engaging all students in IWB activity to develop their thinking) and on how you might refine your lessons
- sharing new ideas and practices with colleagues.

1.4 Deciding where to start

Having considered the components of the resource, how you use it is of course a matter for your professional judgement, probably in consultation with the colleagues that you plan to work with in your institution. However, there do seem to be three possible broad starting points, depending upon your existing understanding of a dialogic approach and your current use of the IWB in the classroom. The following self-evaluation statement sets should help you to decide on an appropriate starting point for you and your colleagues. Read through each set, considering which is most appropriate to your circumstances, and then follow the suggested starting point.

Statement set 1

- I am not entirely sure what the distinctions are between classroom dialogue and classroom talk.
- I am unsure what a 'dialogic classroom' might look like.
- I would value the chance to talk through issues about classroom talk and dialogue with my colleagues.
- I would appreciate the opportunity to review a video example of classroom dialogue 'in action'.

If these statements broadly reflect your position you should 'start at the very beginning', with Section 2.1.

Statement set 2

- I am fairly comfortable with the idea of dialogue, as distinct from talk.
- I would be interested in auditing my own practice in line with a conception of the 'dialogic classroom', before considering where the IWB 'fits' in developing classroom dialogue.

If these statements broadly reflect your position you should probably start with Section 2c.

Statement set 3

- I feel completely comfortable with ideas and issues relating to the whole notion of the 'dialogic classroom'.
- I am primarily interested in examining the role that the IWB has to play in supporting my own well-established dialogic practice.

If these statements broadly reflect your position you should probably start with Section 2d.

2 Stimuli for professional development

Each of these stimuli is really intended to get you talking with your colleagues, but of course if you are doing this alone you should record, in some way, your conclusions for each section. Whether working individually or collaboratively, we suggest that you might like to literally record your thoughts and conclusions on a voice recorder, so that when you have completed your work on the resource you can listen back in order to assess how your thinking has developed.

2.1 Getting started

Reflection

Discuss, or reflect, on:

- How do you currently use talk in lessons?
- How important is a focus on talk?
- What barriers are there to using talk as a tool for learning?
- What do you currently understand by the terms 'dialogue' and 'dialogic' teaching?

In doing this, you will need to consider the various contexts for talk that occur in the classroom. If you are working with others, make sure that everyone in the group has the opportunity to contribute to the discussion, then use Appendix A1 to see whether you raised the issues that are included there (of course, you may have raised other points and other uses of classroom talk, so see this not as a comprehensive or 'correct' list but as a basis on which to make initial comparisons).

To what extent do your considerations reflect the view expressed by Simon Knight in Part B (see Reader, Chapter 1, p. 30)?

> Classroom talk . . . tends to focus on an individual, and for the majority of the time this individual is the teacher. Furthermore, there is a rather unequal balance in classroom communication, with particular rights, and expectations – including the expectation to confer or affirm 'correct' answers – placed on the teacher. Teachers commonly use talk to assess understanding, both of classes and individuals (but) there is a temptation not to explore beyond the individual pupil's answer . . . nor the reasoning and further understanding behind it.

2.2 What is dialogue?

Dialogue is more than just 'talk'. It:

- involves teachers and learners commenting and *cumulatively* building on each other's ideas, posing questions and constructing interpretations together (Alexander 2008)
- means seeing things from someone else's perspective
- is characterized by chains of (open) questions and answers
- may be sustained over the course of a single lesson or across lessons
- builds on the notion of 'exploratory talk' – learners construct shared knowledge and are willing to change their minds and critique their own ideas (Mercer 2000).

All of these things, then, characterize dialogue as a particular way of interacting through talk. If you think back to your work for '2.1 Getting started' you can see that it is talk with a very distinct character and purpose, designed to enable people to 'interthink' (Mercer 2000) and come to an understanding of one another's knowledge and perspectives.

It is worth noting here that spoken dialogue can be assisted by non-verbal elements. We will all have experience of saying 'let me show you what I mean' and then doing something that contributes to a spoken exchange of understanding. This is important here, since in the context of using the IWB students do not always articulate their reasoning verbally; they may do something on the board that reflects their understanding of an idea or of the perspectives presented through spoken dialogue. Thus, dialogue can be non-verbal too!

Why is dialogue a 'good thing'?

Dialogue can take up lesson time but research confirms its long-term value for student learning: enhancing dialogic interaction in the classroom has been shown to enhance both reasoning skills and subject attainment. Importantly, it can lead to longer-term development of conceptual understanding well after a dialogic interaction has taken place. This is because dialogic interactions often provide a starting point for students in thinking about and revising their own understanding. Having considered the views of others and expressed the reasoning behind their pre-existing ideas, students reflect further on how ideas are different and will often continue to develop ideas long after the interaction has occurred.

Here is another extract from Simon Knight's chapter later in this resource (see p. 30) that considers the links between dialogic classroom practices and student attainment:

> [T]he dialogue used to create 'common knowledge' is related to the educational development of children. Indeed, the strong consensus is that high quality dialogue is associated with learning . . . Engaging children in extended talk which encourages them to 'interthink' and explain themselves – as in the Thinking Together approach – stimulates both their subject learning, and general reasoning skills . . .), as well as their social and language skills . . .

(In the chapter, Simon provides corroborative references for these claims.)

This resource uses examples primarily drawn from work carried out in the classrooms where three of the authors teach: Lloyd's Year 9 history class, Caroline's Year 7 English class and Diane's Year 6 primary class. Students in these classrooms valued lessons in which the IWB and dialogue were explicitly used as complementary tools to enhance learning. For example, Figure A1 shows some of the things Caroline's students said about classroom dialogue.

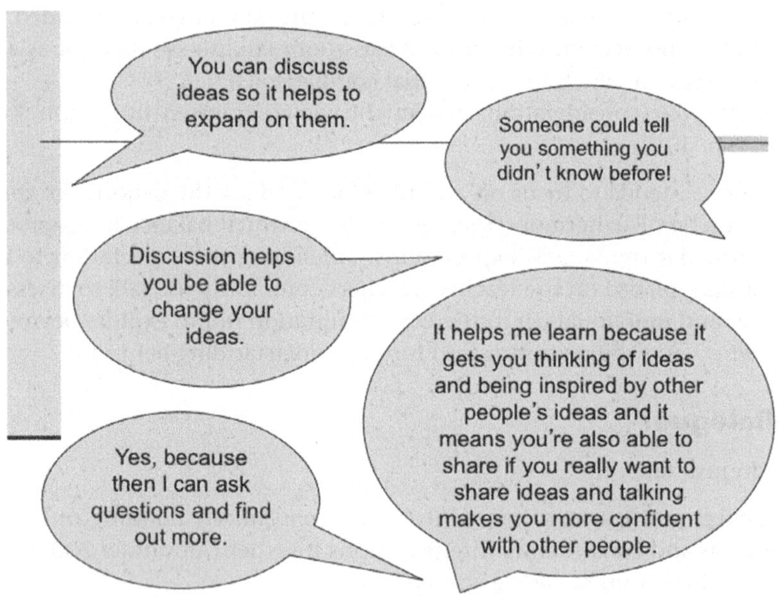

Figure A1 Views of Caroline's students

Once again, Simon Knight's chapter later in this resource (see p. 30) provides an overview of teacher considerations when creating a supportive environment for classroom dialogue:

> With respect to direct pedagogical functions (as opposed to social functions such as behaviour management), dialogue seems to serve several purposes:
>
> 1. supporting individuals' subject learning
> 2. supporting psychological development – the development of oral language and reasoning skills
> 3. promoting whole-class and small-group understanding or commonality
> 4. enabling sharing of ideas that can be improved together (both whole class and small group) – a purpose the IWB is particularly well placed to serve, as later readings discuss.

It will immediately be apparent that the idea of promoting classroom dialogue for learning is rooted in ideas of social and active learning. Essentially, at the heart of the dialogic approach are two core ideas: that we know more collectively than we do individually and benefit from sharing our diverse understandings, and that actively engaging students in their own learning is likely to lead to enhanced learning outcomes.

These ideas chime very strongly with established assessment for learning (AfL) practices in the UK, and you are likely to be familiar with the five core strategies of AfL:

1. Sharing clear learning intentions/objectives for lessons with students
2. Sharing and negotiating lesson success criteria
3. Embedding AfL strategies in lessons and in pupil tasks, to encourage students to express their ideas about what they are learning and what helps them to learn
4. Facilitating peer and self-assessment
5. Encouraging pupil responses to feedback and marking that includes individual target setting.

A dialogic approach has been seen by some as an 'AfL pedagogy', since underpinning all of these AfL strategies is the importance of the structured sharing of ideas and responses to work as part of the process of promoting learning. As we have seen, however, for this to be true the dialogue around classroom activities must have certain elements – it should involve teachers and students commenting and cumulatively building on each other's ideas, posing questions and constructing interpretations together; it may be sustained over the course of a single lesson or across lessons; and it is likely to encourage students to change their minds and critique their own ideas and, if appropriate, to change their minds, in constructing shared knowledge.

Reading 1

Now would be a good time to read Simon Knight's entire chapter in this resource:

- Chapter 1: Creating a supportive environment for classroom dialogue (Simon Knight)

2.3 Considering classroom dialogue

Take a look at the Dialogue Table (Appendix A2) illustrating what classroom dialogue may look like in the context of IWB use. In order to structure teacher thinking about classroom practice it uses the headings 'In my classroom, we:', 'You will see us:' and 'So that we can:'.

As we have seen from Simon Knight's chapter, the classroom climate needs to support dialogue if it is to happen. Look at the first column in the Dialogue Table for more information about this and teachers' underlying intentions. The second column illustrates what kinds of things teachers and learners might do in a dialogic classroom. The third column shows the goals-what dialogic activity could lead to.

Getting to the point where activity in a classroom reflects this Dialogue Table requires structured guidance from the teacher; this includes modelling and careful choice of when a dialogic approach is appropriate in moving learning forward in the classroom (as we have said, when and whether dialogic approaches are to be used is a choice for the teacher, part of their wider pedagogic repertoire). It will be apparent that dialogue does not just happen, any more than productive collaboration does when students work in groups. 'Dialogic teaching' means engaging students in articulating, justifying and evaluating their own points of view; it involves teachers in open-ended questioning, feeding in ideas, reflecting and interpreting; and it offers opportunities for students to become the experts and respond to suggestions or questions posed by their peers. But without the teacher having these as intentions in their classrooms, effective dialogue for learning simply won't happen.

As Caroline Neale says in her chapter later in this resource (Reader, Chapter 3 on developing a dialogic approach to IWB use in English see p. 49):

> For effective dialogue to take place, regardless of resources used to promote it, classroom climate and the establishment of ground rules and agreed ways of working are paramount. Just as students need support with how to read and write effectively, they also require support with the structures for effective and meaningful talk.

Now look at the expanded dialogue table (Appendix A3) with teacher guidance added in two columns (in bold italic font) to illustrate some of the ways teachers could address adopting a dialogic approach. This table came out of work that teacher Diane Rawlins carried out with her staff, and in Chapter 2 in the Reader Diane explains how it was developed (see p. 43):

> Staff need a shared understanding of what dialogue in the classroom looks like; my version of the Expanded Dialogue Table, annotated with guidance and ideas from team discussions, could be a useful way of ensuring this happens. Teaching Assistants also need to be a part of this understanding, so that they can support the dialogic approach effectively.

Dialogue Table Activity 1: Seeing dialogue in action

Just as even the most dialogic teacher's repertoire will include a range of other modes of communication too, no discussion will ever be wholly dialogic. Here is a transcript of a discussion that includes 'rich dialogue' though, to illustrate what this kind of communication is like in practice.

Dialogue from a science lesson on the characteristics of life

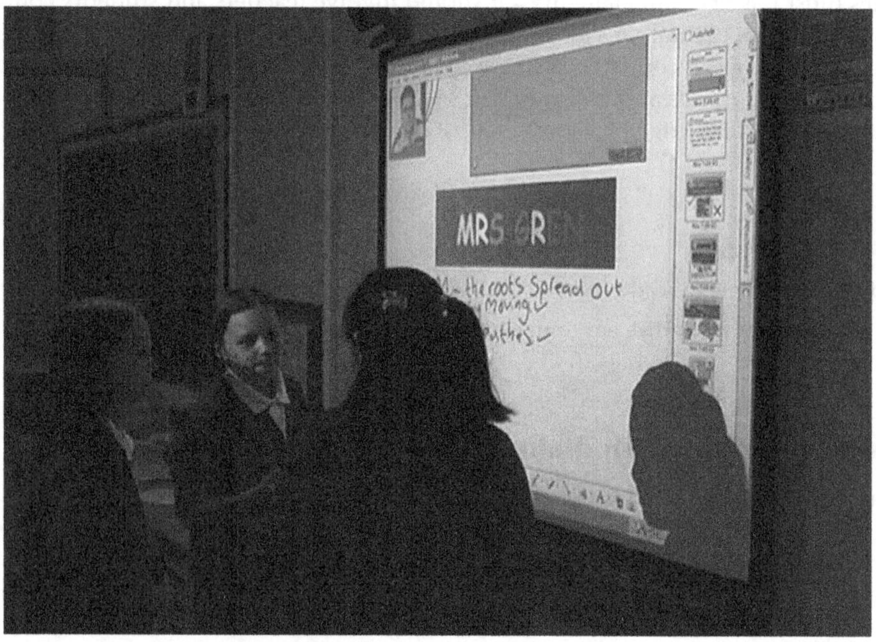

The participants are a mixed ability group of three girls, aged 10 (one student with English as an additional language). The students have seen an animated video about plant growth, reproduction and pollination on the IWB. They are working at the IWB, recording their thoughts about the characteristics of life displayed by plants by scrolling down the IWB page under the video and making notes. The teacher intervenes at one point.

S3:	So does it do reproduction?
S1:	Yeah.
S2:	Yeah because, uh, the seeds grow.
S3:	The seeds get spread out.
S2:	And then they spread out, it's like with a helicopter tree, sycamore.
S3:	Oh right yeah.
S2:	They go all the way to the floor and then the wind goes and blows them away.
S3:	So do we think we should rub that bit out and put in the bit about seeds?
S2:	Yeah, I think so.
S3:	Then I'll take my turn afterwards, yeah?
S1:	Yeah.
Teacher:	Just listening to you, is there anything you know from what we've done this term that you can use here?

S1: This one reproducts because, um, a bee flies from one plant to another.
S3: That's the pollen. What's the word? We did it the other day?
S2: That's pollination.
S3: But the seeds get spread out. How does it go with that?
S2: Because the flower turns into seed.
S1: The seed, the seed is inside the flower, isn't it?
S3: Actually the pollen gets made into the seed, into a seed. It goes into the ovary and then gets made into a seed, and then gets spread out. Do you remember?
S1: So if you see like one poppy there wouldn't be any other poppies around it, there would just be one and one.
S2: And pollen comes along and makes the seed. Is that right? Do we agree?
S1: Yeah.
S3: Yeah.
S2: So, we know it reproducts because....
S1: Because otherwise there would only be one of each plant in the world.
S3: Yeah, that's it.

This excerpt illustrates the idea that dialogic elements of interaction can be woven into broader classroom talk. Notice also that it is not just about what is said by students; the teacher needs to use an inclusive approach and create an atmosphere where children feel safe to contribute their ideas. Although not explicit in this particular excerpt it is certainly implicit.

Task 1

Read the transcript twice, the first time simply to absorb what's going on. Then, use Appendix A2 (Dialogue Table), column 2, as a checklist:

- Which of these practices are evident in the excerpt?
- Are there other elements of the interaction that seem to be significant? How would you define them?
- Can you sum up, on paper or with colleagues, why this example does or doesn't illustrate classroom dialogue (as opposed to just talk)?

Dialogue Table Activity 2: does my own teaching support dialogue?

Task 2

'Audit' your practice using the Expanded Dialogue Table (Appendix A3). Do you do some or all of this now?

This exercise probably needs to be carried out individually as a reflective activity at first. It would then be useful to share your conclusions with one or more colleagues or, even better, have a colleague review one of your lessons using the table; this will allow you to compare your own views with the evidence from external observation.

Having done this work, look at column 1 again. Is the ethos in your classroom supportive of dialogue? How could you make it more supportive? Again, Diane Rawlins chapter is useful here; in this extract he briefly considers the creation of classroom 'talk rules' and stresses the importance of planning for dialogue (see p. 42).

> [G]iving explicit guidance on talk and how we can work together on talk-based tasks is important, so that all children understand their role in the learning. The rules also reassure children, provided they are backed up by good-quality practice in the classroom, that their input is valued and valuable in our learning . . .

Planning should include opportunities for talk which are not just focused on getting the 'right answer', but may involve speculating, questioning, criticizing and building new understandings of concepts. This must be backed up by skilled teacher intervention in modelling and prompting children to question each other's ideas and views, e.g. 'X, what do you think about Y's idea?'

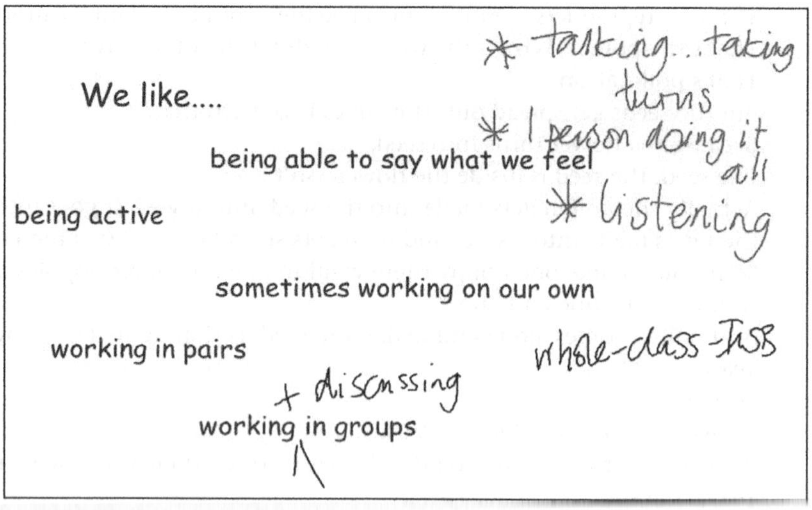

Figure A2 Devising talk rules

Videos 1 and 2

It is useful to look at a video clip that supports what Simon is saying and two examples of introducing and using talk rules, as in Diane's classroom, can be found online at: http://tinyurl.com/OUPIWB.

(For much more on the creating of classroom talk rules, see the free downloadable classroom materials at http://www.thinking-together.org.uk/.)

Task 3

(Associated with a review of your practice and Videos 1 and 2)
Consider:

- Would you revise or add anything to the table?
- Are there any barriers to promoting dialogue in your setting? How can you overcome any barriers to learning?
- What are your initial thoughts about how you might like to develop a more 'dialogic' approach? Record at least one idea.

Reading 2

Now is a good point at which to read the following two chapters in Part B:

- Chapter 2: Supporting dialogic teaching of personal safety with the interactive whiteboard in an urban primary school (Diane Rawlins)
- Chapter 3: Developing a dialogic approach to interactive whiteboard use in English: teacher reflections and student perceptions (Caroline Neale)

2.4 What role can the IWB play in supporting whole-class dialogue?

In considering the work that Caroline Neale (Part B, Chapter 3) carried out in her own classroom as part of our collective IWB project, she notes:

> The key aspects of IWB use that stand out in this project are: firstly, its 'motivational' and 'engaging' characteristics, and secondly its role in sustaining the continuity of dialogue and learning over sequences of lessons. In terms of supporting teaching and learning, the IWB software means that resources can be prepared in advance, allowing for a faster pace in lessons. Some may argue that this could prevent spontaneity and flexibility, however, the adaptability of the IWB comes into play here: for example, its ability to move forward or back through slides as many times as necessary, amending and adding new slides if required, obviates the

need for a 'fixed' lesson plan. The other feature which I have found invaluable and which has also been commented on by students is the fact that work from lessons can be saved and then used again or referred back to in future lessons, and this function can be used both within and across teaching groups.

So let us now consider the use of the IWB for dialogic teaching purposes.

Reading 3

Throughout this next section, links are made to the ideas that appear in the following chapter in Part B:

- Chapter 5: Supporting dialogue by exploiting interactive features of the IWB (Sara Hennessy)

You might like to read this now, or after the section, and to think about how you might like to use these features of the IWB in your own setting.

The chapter points out:

(a) That the specialized tools for directly manipulating digital objects that are provided through the IWB software offer significant 'added value' in exploring ideas, supporting reasoning and drawing attention to salient features of a representation or process. For example, they include tools for annotating text or images, highlighting, drawing, hide-and-reveal, resizing and zooming (Figure A3).

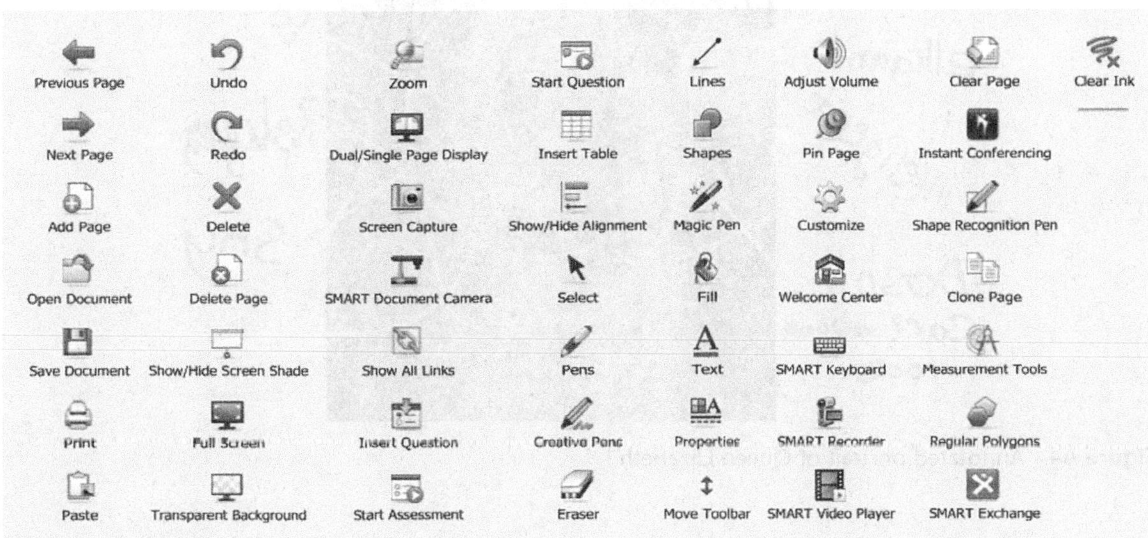

Figure A3 SMART Notebook tools

(b) That the IWB also allows *multimodal* interaction with a wide range of digital media resources.

These include texts, photographs, multimedia presentations, animations, simulations and models, interactive diagrams, spread sheets and databases, graphs and charts, tables, web pages, maps, audio and video files, etc. Using such visual and dynamic representations helps to make complex subject concepts and processes more explicit, concrete and transparent . . . because they are usually publicly interpreted through teachers' and students' speech, gaze and gesture . . . [offering] opportunities to check understanding and supply clarification.

(c) That 'digital artefacts' – objects or texts collaboratively produced, manipulated and refined by teachers and students – can play a pivotal role in supporting ongoing dialogues and knowledge building. They visibly represent the knowledge that is developing in the class and make differences between perspectives more explicit; dialogues develop around interaction with them.

IWB activity 1

Read through the task below and then watch, either individually or with colleagues, two examples of using the IWB to support dialogue in a whole class context. In all of these tasks, dialogue between you and your colleagues is desirable, so that everyone's perspectives can be aired. If you are working alone, ensure that you create a reflective commentary on each task and return to review these when all of the tasks are completed.

Video 3

The first example considers a class annotating a portrait of Queen Elizabeth. You will find the clip at http://tinyurl.com/OUPIWB. This 9-minute clip depicts students aged 13–14 in turn annotating a digital photograph of a historical portrait (of the young Queen Elizabeth I) projected onto the IWB (Figure A4). (It comes from a sequence of six lessons portrayed in more detail at http://t-media.educ.cam.ac.uk/; these lessons were taught by Lloyd Brown, one of the authors of this resource, and recorded during an earlier research project, 'T-MEDIA'). You may wish to watch it more than once.

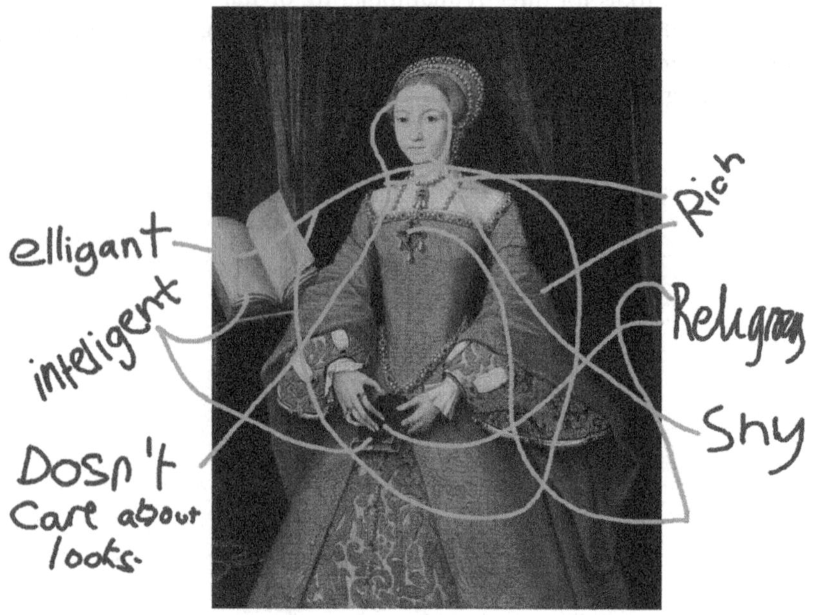

Figure A4 Annotated portrait of Queen Elizabeth I

> **Task 4**
>
> (Associated with Video 3)
>
> *Before* you read the commentary below, watch the clip and consider some or all of these core questions that inform this part of the resource:
>
> - How did the teacher support dialogue?
> - How did the teacher weave the use of the IWB into the lesson activities?
> - Would you in fact define what is happening here as broadly dialogic?
> - What features of the teacher and student talk and actions could be characterized as dialogic?
> - What would you say are the 'critical incidents' for students' understanding in this lesson segment?
> - Is dialogue, as we have now defined it, the only type of talk taking place here?
> - Does this clip mirror any elements of your own practice?
> - What messages for your own practice are contained in this clip? Discuss how useful/feasible these activities and strategies are in your own setting.

Commentary

This clip shows students being asked to interpret their peers' thinking by drawing links between features of the image and descriptive labels around the picture that others had already written without comment. This activity developed a collective, enhanced understanding of the 'Golden Age' of Elizabeth I, maximizing the number of students that could interact directly with the portrait. The teacher, Lloyd, then built upon the students' interpretations in the plenary discussion by subtly helping them to understand Elizabeth's motives and subsequent events. He created continuity of dialogue over time by comparing the portrait with a previously displayed one of the older Elizabeth. He questioned the 'reality' portrayed by any historical artefact, concluding both that pictures only tell a partial story and that his own ideas had been changed by the activity. In this democratic classroom, the teacher was also a learner.

IWB activity 2

Video 4

Now consider a clip from a primary school lesson on keeping secrets, illustrating use of open-ended prompts, an image and audio recordings by children (aged 10) to stimulate discussion (Figure A5). It can be found at http://tinyurl.com/OUPIWB. This 3-minute clip comes from the lesson sequence described and reflected upon by teacher Diane Rawlins in Part B, Reader, Chapter 2.

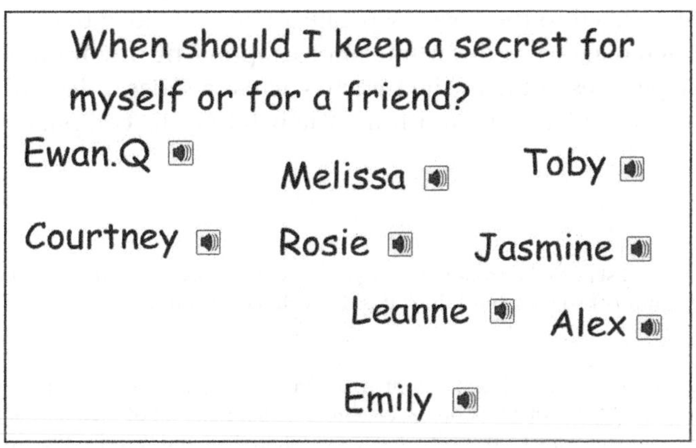

Figure A5 Stored audio recordings of students' views

> **Task 5**
>
> (Associated with Video 4)
>
> Again, *before* reading the commentary, watch the clip and consider the core questions that you considered when evaluating IWB activity 1.

Commentary

This clip shows an introduction to the whole issue of keeping secrets. Diane uses a single image to stimulate some initial discussion, with a ticker-tape 'core' question streaming across the screen. She then uses sound files, recorded before the lesson, to give the children 'another voice' through which they can express their ideas and which can then act as a stimulus for continuing dialogue. This is another way of sharing views orally. It is easiest to do using the IWB's own audio recording facility – even young primary children can operate this themselves – but can be done using a portable digital audio recorder too. Playing pre-recordings of students' opinions is an effective stimulus for class dialogue – it pre-packages the information for discussion, and encourages students to respond to each other. Audio files can be embedded in the flipchart so they can easily be clicked on to play in succession. As Diane says in her Reader chapter:

> I recorded myself reading a text to be used in the second lesson, and I was able to observe the children's reactions whilst they were hearing the text for the first time. I could not have done this had I been reading the text to them. Additionally, children were very motivated by recording their own views straight onto the flipchart pages; it is very simple to do, and they can revisit earlier views by listening to them again, potentially noting where their thinking has changed as a result of subsequent learning.

Before we continue, it is important to notice that quite straightforward uses of the IWB can be effective; you don't need to be a technical whizz to use the IWB as a tool for promoting classroom dialogue!

IWB activity 3: Exploring trench warfare using multimedia resources

Video 5

This activity uses a 2-minute subtitled compilation of clips from two secondary history lessons, in which a variety of resources (including a doctor's war diary: Figure A6) were used to build up dialogue and guide inquiry over time; the focus for the work was the open-ended question: 'Can we imagine the experience of trench warfare?' While the compilation gives a flavour of the work, it is important to note that, though they are not depicted, other IWB resources were used during the lesson sequence; these included a poem, a YouTube video related to the poem, separate audio and video tracks of a trench warfare film on DVD, a textbook trench diagram and wartime photographs. The intention was to conjure up different experiences and perspectives of life in the trenches across a series of lessons, raising the important point that dialogue can connect learning over time. You will find the compilation clip at http://tinyurl.com/OUPIWB.

If I ever get sent to the front with a regiment, I shall shed tears of joy. I do envy Chris going off so soon but I think this dog will have his day soon too.

We expect to be moved to the front at any moment. The men apparently will be in the trenches alternate 24 hours, changing with a fresh lot of men during the night. I am behind HQ, probably a dug out where I sit and wait for the wounded to be brought to me. I am told that doctors are not allowed in the trenches. I am told that the feeding at the front is splendid and there is a Daily Mail for every 10 men.

Our men have had a terrible experience of 24 hours in trenches, drenched through and in some places knee deep in mud and water. To see them come out, line up and march off is almost terrible. They don't look like strong young men. They are muddied to the eyes. Their coats are plastered with mud and weigh an awful lot with the water that has soaked in. Their backs are bent and they stagger and totter along with the weight of their packs. Their faces are white and haggard and their faces glare out from mud. They look like wounded, sick, wild things. Many, too many who are quite beat are told they must walk it. Then comes the nightmare of a march of 2 to 4 miles which they do in a trance.

Figure A6 Underlining key phrases in doctor's war diary

Task 6

(Associated with Video 5)

Again, *before* reading the commentary, watch the clip and consider the core questions that you considered when evaluating IWB Activities 1 and 2.

Commentary

This compilation of clips is taken from two history lessons with a class of boys aged 12–13. It illustrates how together they explored over time the open-ended question: 'Can we imagine the experience of trench warfare?' Interactive whiteboard activities were interspersed with 'talk pairs' and class discussions. The teacher, Lloyd, employed a very wide range of multimedia resources, beginning with whole class interpretation of an army doctor's 1914 diary text, revealed in stages using the IWB's hide-and-reveal tool. One boy used the IWB's underlining tool to identify key phrases in the text and explained his reasoning to the class. Students then worked in pairs to co-construct a video storyboard on mini wipe-clean whiteboards; the compilation shows one pair explaining theirs at the IWB and the class then discussing the boys' ideas. The cumulative nature of the work is interesting here, as there is evidence that one function of dialogue can be to disrupt pre-existing ideas, forcing the learner to reconsider their perspectives over time (Littleton and Howe 2010). In this sequence, the series of interrelated IWB resources used helped to underpin a dialogue that was cumulative over time. Notice too how the teacher places himself at the back of the room sometimes.

Task 7

Take a look at Appendix A4, which provides a rich example of resulting dialogue from a plenary discussion in the following (third) lesson in Lloyd's sequence.

Using a copy of this dialogue, highlight the sections that you think represent dialogue, as opposed to other kinds of talk. Look especially for open questions, reasoning that builds on previous speakers' contributions, and see how the teacher allows uncertainty. Do this individually and, if possible, compare your highlighting with that of a colleague.

Reading 4

Now you might like to read:

- Chapter 4: Using the interactive whiteboard to support dialogic teaching in history: the student perspective (Lloyd Brown)

This describes and reflects on not only this lesson sequence but his work in developing dialogic teaching and learning across his department and school.

Reading 5

If you haven't done so already, this is also a good point at which to read:

- Chapter 5: Supporting dialogue by exploiting interactive features of the IWB (Sara Hennessy)

Task 8

Sketch out some ideas for an up-coming lesson of your own, considering how you might capitalize on the 'multimodal' nature of the IWB – the way it allows you to use a variety of digital media resources to stimulate dialogue. (This need not necessarily lead to a formal lesson planning activity, which we consider later; you should treat it as a way of considering possibilities.)

2.5 Extending our understanding of IWB use in a dialogic classroom to small-group work and computer-based activity

In all of the lesson sequences illustrated in Section 2.4, the IWB was not continually used, nor was whole-class dialogue the only kind that took place. You will also notice that the teachers' intentions and actions in columns 1 and 2 of the Dialogue Tables may or may not involve the IWB or other technologies. Most teachers have a very varied pedagogical repertoire, which we have already alluded to. We view the IWB as the central resource – the technological hub – within a *dialogic classroom space* constructed by the teacher, who creates a supportive ethos for dialogue. The teacher engages students in a variety of carefully planned forms of dialogic interaction and activity; these are located away from as well as at the board. They may intentionally precede or follow up activity involving the IWB, including, for example, reflection on what the class has created on the IWB or on projected resources. Dialogic teaching in the context of IWB use typically includes a mixture of whole-class teaching, individual and small-group work. In some contexts, IWB use itself may even involve *small groups working at the board without the teacher present*; this atypical situation has been researched by Paul Warwick, Neil Mercer and their colleagues, as we now illustrate.

IWB activity 4: Small-group work at the IWB

In Chapter 6, Paul Warwick considers the use of the IWB by primary school students working in groups. He says:

> We may intend that children should make an active contribution to class and group interaction and we may have a classroom ethos that is accepting of children expressing their understandings; but unless we give them the tools to do so, their interactions are likely to be less productive than they might otherwise have been. Thus we must address students' general lack of awareness of the crucial importance of talk for learning. They need to know that there are different kinds of talk and they need a clear understanding that talk for learning involves engaging one another in the sort of discussion that will help everyone to do better than each could alone.
>
> However, students also need to be given something interesting to talk about. Tasks need to be conceptually engaging and, if the intention is to promote the kind of dialogue that reveals understanding, tasks should be structured in such a way that students are required to interact and to talk productively. It is here that the IWB has much to offer. As a classroom tool it has been widely used by teachers to extend their 'pedagogic repertoires', the diverse strategies that all teachers have in their armoury and employ as appropriate . . . But many teachers are looking at the potential of the IWB as more than a 'teacher resource box' . . . So what is it about the IWB that seems to lend itself to semi-autonomous group work, and where are there examples of such work?

Task 9

(Associated with videos 6 and 7)
Take a look at the two video clips below and consider the questions about each one.

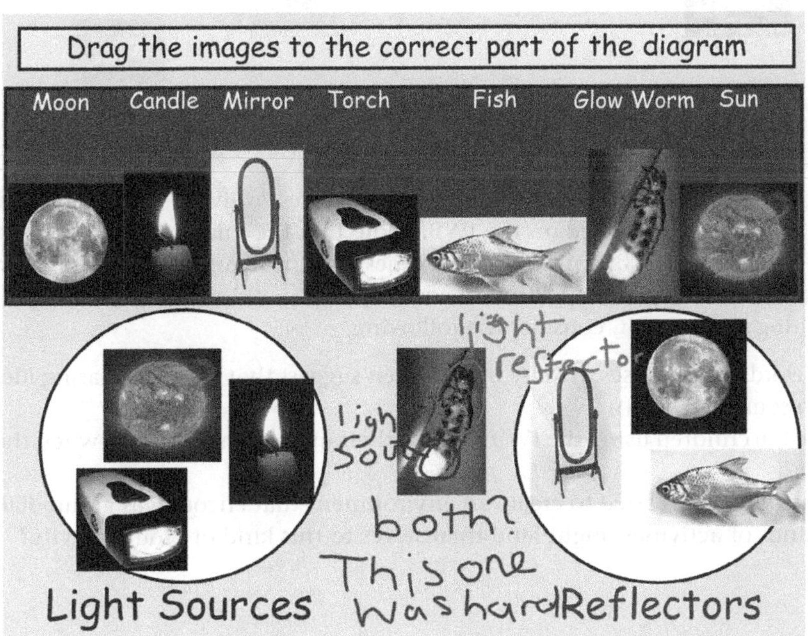

Video 6

In the first clip, the students are considering where to place an image of a glow worm under the required categories of light reflector and light emitter. You will find the clip at http://tinyurl.com/OUPIWB.

When watching this clip, consider the following:

- How has the teacher structured the work on the screen to ensure that the children talk to one another?
- What evidence is there from the children's talk that they are supporting one another in their thinking?
- In what ways do the children use the IWB as part of the dialogue, to express and communicate their understanding?
- Would there be a place for similar group work in your classroom?

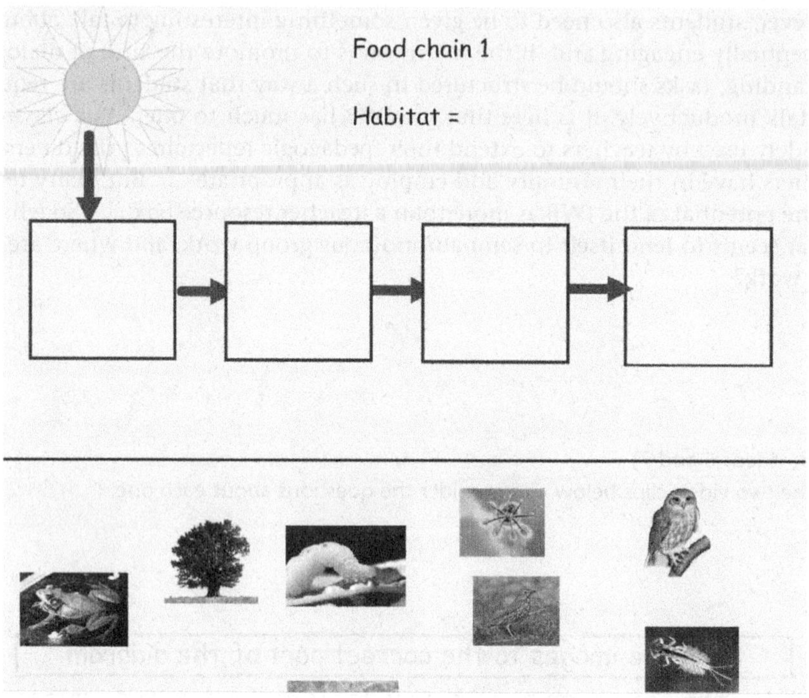

Video 7

In the second clip the students are required to select pictures of living things and place them into a food chain that has been constructed on the IWB. (Note that the images have been hyperlinked by the teacher to descriptions of each organism; this becomes a slight inconvenience for the students, as you will see). You will find the clip at http://tinyurl.com/OUPIWB.

When watching this excerpt, consider the following:

- Which words and phrases used by the children suggest that they are sharing ideas and trying to come to some agreement?
- How are the children using the IWB to show their understanding, even when they don't express it in words?
- How has the teacher tried to create an environment that encourages group dialogue?
- What kinds of activities might lend themselves to this kind of group activity?

Reading 6

To learn more about supporting independent group work with the IWB you should now read:

- Chapter 6: Effective group work at the interactive whiteboard (Paul Warwick)

You may also like more information about the classroom research that informed the chapter – if so, go to http://iwbcollaboration.educ.cam.ac.uk/.

Supporting dialogue through computer-based activity

The IWB can also be used in conjunction with other computer-based group activities, and the latter (with or without the IWB) can support dialogue if children 'learn how to learn together' a key twenty-first-century learning skill. In the Reader, Chapter 7, Rupert Wegerif describes how teachers can harness collaborative uses of technology to help children in learning subject matter, developing skills for dialogue and actually 'becoming aware of all the things that make learning together with others in groups work'. He argues that 'technology like the Internet supports learning together with others even when the group are not altogether in the same place'.

Rupert points out that the same teacher strategies and changes in the role of the teacher and the culture of the class mentioned in the sections above are relevant in this group work context. He offers a number of strategies directly aimed at supporting learning to learn with others in groups, for example distributed leadership, encouraging group reflection and using the language of reasoning, including modelling disagreement. The chapter illustrates these in the context of email interaction and Internet searching – with and without the IWB.

Reading 7

To consider how computer-based tasks might be supported in your setting via the interactive uses of the IWB described earlier read:

- Chapter 7: Learning to learn together with ICT and with the Internet (Rupert Wegerif)

How can you create a supportive classroom climate for dialogue in this context? The work you have done with Chapters 1 and 5 will help your thinking here.

2.6 Using the Resource Bank – more ideas for using the IWB

> None of the activities devised was technologically complicated, but for me, this is just one of the benefits of the IWB – the simplest of uses can be extremely effective. (Caroline Neale, Reader, Chapter 3)

The video clips that you have been dipping into for the earlier IWB activities are part of a collection of further clips. All of the clips are linked to a wider, online Resource Bank that accompanies this resource and which can again be accessed at http://tinyurl.com/OUPIWB. It contains short descriptions of various examples of IWB activities, illustrated with colour screen shots and/or video clips in each case.

Here we give you an example of one activity, just to give you an idea of what the Resource Bank contains. The activities are often linked to IWB flipchart templates (provided as separate Resource Bank files in SMART Notebook and ActivInspire format) that can be used to create your own versions. The materials collectively show different uses of the IWB for dialogic teaching and learning – starting with really simple ideas and moving on to 'fancier' ways of using the board. They also illustrate or describe the teacher's role in promoting dialogue in each case.

Sample Resource Bank activity: Model mapping/mind mapping
Students use key terms and drag and drop words/draw arrows/add text to make connections and explain key ideas about a topic. Results can be saved and added to throughout a lesson/topic of work. Learners could make a mind map at their desks before or during the class activity, or they could do the activity at the beginning and end of a lesson or lesson sequence to illustrate to themselves and the teacher what they have learned. This is especially useful for children with literacy difficulties.

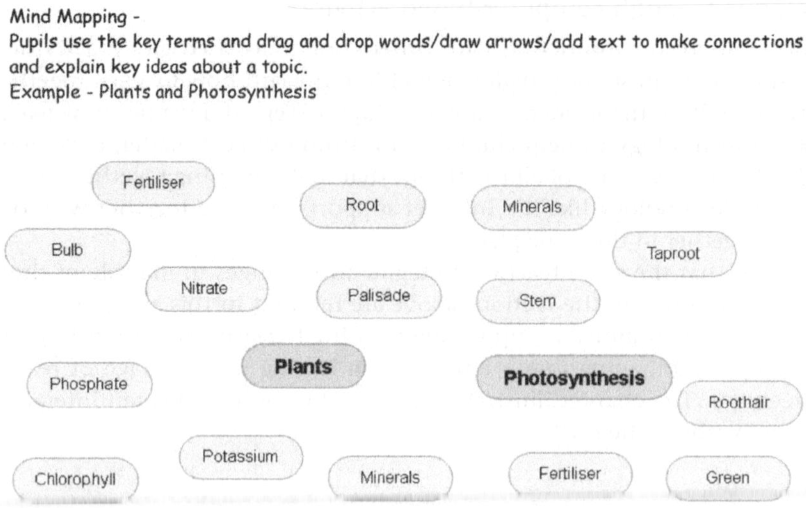

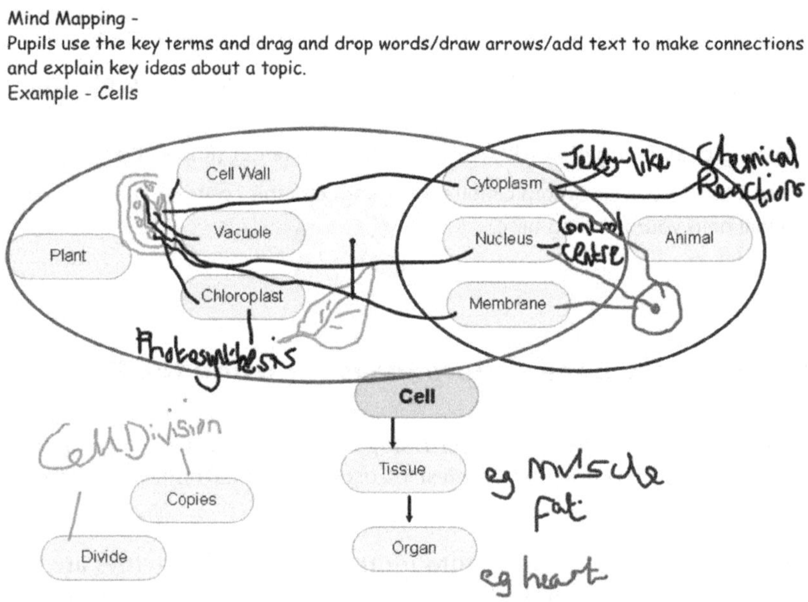

see Template, Mind Map

The Resource Bank also contains the actual flipcharts prepared for the lessons described by the teachers who authored Chapters 2–4 in Part B, Reader.

You should now feel equipped with the knowledge, questions and strategies to make the most of viewing these resources, either individually or with colleagues, or as part of a staff development programme.

Task 10

As you view the various activities summarized in the Resource Bank and the further videos and templates linked to some of them, consider:

- Are any of these ideas useful to you?
- In what other ways, and contexts, might they be applied or adapted?
- What might be effective with your particular students?
- Which activities might lend themselves to group work rather than whole class work?

Imagine you had seen a colleague teaching in the way depicted in each video clip; what feedback would you give them? How would you suggest they might enhance their practice? In doing this, don't forget to use the Dialogue Tables (Appendices A2 and A3) where appropriate.

2.7 Reviewing your learning – consolidating what you have done so far and preparing for planning your own lessons

Task 11: Reviewing teacher strategies for supporting dialogue

Skim read Resource Appendices A5–7. They provide some concrete ideas and re-iterate a framework of understanding as a basis on which to plan your lesson. Then consider them in more depth in relation to the points a–c which follow.

(a) Creating a climate for dialogue

As we have suggested, students need to feel at ease within their classroom community if they are to participate in dialogue. Opinions vary between teachers as to how important 'hands-on' use of the IWB by students is for learning. Adolescents, in particular, may be quite self-conscious and hence reluctant to come up to the IWB in case they make a 'mistake'. Appendix A5 summarizes on one handy page some of the actions you can take to make students feel comfortable enough in the classroom to engage in dialogue. It builds on the material above and some further ideas in listing steps for creating a supportive learning community and for 'scaffolding'[1] learning within that community.

In the context of these comments you may wish to skim read again Reader, Chapter 1 by Simon Knight and Chapter 7 by Rupert Wegerif. The latter indicates that many classroom tasks that are carried out at individual computers, such as Internet search tasks in pairs or groups, can emphasize dialogue more than otherwise may be the case in many classrooms. As we have seen, using the IWB as well can enhance this:

> The IWB can play a key role in teaching children to use the Internet efficiently. The teacher can model effective searching using the Internet live on the screen, and can facilitate a dialogue around interpreting the outcomes of searches, again using the language of reasoning. Web-based educational resources such as online videos, simulations and animations can also be played live and spontaneously according to the direction of a discussion.

(b) Teacher strategies for supporting dialogue with the IWB

Appendix A6 lists some of the main strategies that teachers can use to support dialogue with the IWB.

You have considered your own practice and that of others, looking at some of the IWB-based strategies that might be used to promote dialogue. Does Appendix A6 add to your store of potential strategies? Which ones would you like to try, and why?

(c) Engaging all students in IWB activity

Hands-on use of the IWB by learners is often motivating, but can become mundane unless it is carefully orchestrated; cognitive involvement by the students must also be prioritized. In Chapter 5 of the Reader, Sara Hennessy offers examples of how teachers engage all learners in IWB-based activity, including:

> [S]tudents working on arranging their own paper mini-diagrams that replicate the IWB image (e.g. composing the photosynthesis equation or matching terms and definitions/functions), justifying their own arrangements to peers. One learner could then arrange the ideas on the IWB with others verifying the arrangement. Prediction could engage a whole class, as in the science lesson described earlier, where students worked with peers to formulate a theory about how the structural features of alveoli facilitate gaseous exchange.

In your classroom are there opportunities for peers to give input or feedback when another student is at the board? How can you avoid those in their seats merely being spectators? Would individual or paired work on mini-whiteboards or in exercise books be useful here? Can students verify or make input into what their peer at the board is doing?

Appendix A7 offers some of Lloyd Brown's own suggestions about how you can get all students to participate, including activities for those who don't get a chance to come up to the IWB in the lesson. Read it carefully now.

Are these useful ideas? Can you think of any others that might work in your context?

Task 12: Trying out a new idea – planning, teaching and reviewing a lesson

Planning

Choose some aspect of what you have learned about a dialogic approach to try out in your classroom. With specific reference to integrating the IWB into the lesson you are considering, you might try something you have seen here or a related idea of your own. Naturally you will start by thinking about addressing your students' particular starting point and needs.

Plan a lesson with a new element drawn from your understanding of this material. You might want to focus on engagement or the learning of a couple of particular students when you evaluate it. The strategies that feature in Reader, Chapters 2–4, might also be helpful to bear in mind and you might like to take a look at the templates provided for IWB activities (in SMART Notebook or Promethean ActivInspire format) in the online Resource Bank at http://tinyurl.com/OUPIWB.

Teaching

Try out your ideas in a lesson and, if possible, get a colleague to observe you and take notes; whether working individually or with a colleague you may wish to video the lesson for review. You might consider using Appendix A2 (Dialogue Table), or your own version of it, as an observation guide.

Reflection checklist

Here we provide a set of prompts and ideas, in the form of questions, to support the lesson review process. Use those that seem most relevant to your context, either individually or with colleagues.

An overview of the lesson

- How did your new element change the rest of the lesson?
- How did/could you integrate IWB use into the lesson, linking it with other activities not involving technology? What kind of individual/pair/group activities were useful to prepare for or to follow up whole class work with the IWB?
- How did the lesson link with the Dialogue Table? (What would you revise/add to the table for your own context?)
- What did you do that helped the activity to promote dialogue?
- How successful was this? Did the students (and you) build on each other's contributions?

Look again at the list of teacher strategies for supporting dialogue with the IWB that appear in Appendix A6:

- Did you use any strategies like these? Would you like to try any of them in future?
- How did students respond? Do they see the value of dialogue? How do you know?
- What would you expect to see next time?
- What problems came up and how did you deal with them?
- What kinds of dialogue took place? Was there any non-verbal dialogue as students interacted with the board?

Learning outcomes

- What were the intended learning outcomes and how can you assess them?
- Are they content or process knowledge?
- What are individuals or small groups taking away from sharing ideas and constructing objects together?
- How might you help the dialogue, reflection and learning to continue over time?

Considering student recording

What students might usefully record of their deliberations during lessons involving dialogue and the IWB takes some thought. It is directly related to 'Engaging all students in IWB activity' above (Section 2.7 and Appendix A7), since one way of getting everyone to participate is using a recording mechanism. Examples observed during our studies include saving annotations and drawings, printing miniature copies of IWB screens for individuals to stick in exercise books and annotate, students recording in their books their own or peers' ideas (from discussion or from the board), or writing down notes or definitions phrased in their own words. Mini-whiteboards can also be used for a less permanent form of recording.

In your lesson:

- Did you revisit any saved slides in order to continue a dialogue?
- Are there other records of anything during the dialogue in your lesson?
- If not, would this be useful in future for students?
- What would you choose to save from this lesson, and why?
- Would it be useful to consider ways in which the dialogue in your lesson could be built upon over time – with the same students or even a different group?

Next time

You are likely to be already considering what you would change next time and what else you would like to try out. One thing that you might consider is canvassing students' views on your developing practice. Appendix A8 briefly describes Lloyd Brown's ideas on how you can find out more about what students think. Two common approaches that he outlines there are the use of a simple questionnaire, or getting a focus group of students to use a flip camera to record their views. You could also interview a group of students at the end of a lesson or at some later date. Lloyd involved students in his research as 'learning partners' and conducted a pupil survey using questionnaires, as he describes in Chapter 4 in the Reader. He gathered some very interesting information through his classroom research study. For example one pupil responded that 'from writing I have learnt most of the facts and dates, but through discussion I have learnt other theories and points of view and seen things from a different angle'. The majority of the class of students canvassed felt they had learned more from discussion than from writing. Although Lloyd's study took place in a history classroom, he believes the findings have implications for teaching in other subject areas. Lloyd reported in his findings section that:

> [T]he learning partners work has made me reassess my own thinking about a 'dialogic lesson' and particularly the role of the teacher within it . . . it seems that this group of students believes that they learned more from discussion than from writing in these lessons . . . some students said that discussion helps their learning because they can 'get ideas from other people'.

Reading 8

Refer back to:

- Chapter 4, Using the interactive whiteboard to support dialogic teaching in history: the student perspective (Lloyd Brown)

Here you can revisit how Lloyd used the multimodal features of the IWB in his lessons and how he gathered students' views in his action research.

2.8 Sharing new ideas

Having worked through all of the material in this resource, you have already been engaging in action research (Figure A7) – looking at your own practice, reflecting on it and developing your practice in new directions.

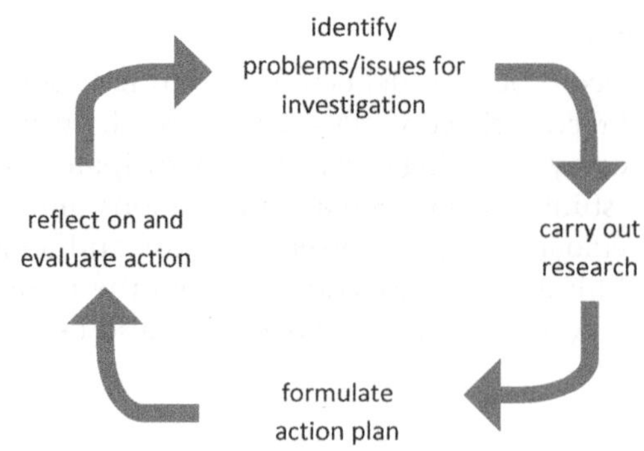

Figure A.7 The action research cycle
Source: From an online resource at http://www.llas.ac.uk/projects/2837, reproduced here by kind permission of John Canning of LLAS Centre for Languages, Linguistics and Area Studies.

But what next, beyond further development of your own practice? Diane (Chapter 2 in the Reader) says:

> For my learning to be truly worthwhile, it must be shared... this opportunity to work on a different plane from my usual, practical-based approach was illuminating in many ways, and I found it refreshing to be working collaboratively to develop definitions of how dialogue would 'look' in our classrooms, and to pinpoint how and for what purposes the IWB was actually being used within a lesson.
>
> (As a staff) we looked at example flipcharts on our network, being interested in the use of images, whether flipcharts were being made simply as a lesson 'script', or whether they had the possibility of being used flexibly as an ongoing record/stimulus/means of review.

Would any of your colleagues be interested in trying out some of the ideas in this resource or hearing about what you did? Could you extend the activity to another year group or department, or another school that you normally work with?

Your institution may be interested to develop an action plan to promote a whole-school approach, for example through dedicated staff meetings. The sample action plan provided in Appendix A9 is aimed at senior leaders and can also be adapted for use by smaller groups or working with other schools/institutions. All three of the teachers involved in developing this resource (including the action plan which was devised by Diane Rawlins) spontaneously instigated a whole-school approach to supporting dialogue in their respective institutions, as mentioned in their Reader chapter accounts. You may also be interested in reading about the related research by Flitton and Warwick (2013) and how it led to whole-school professional development in the area of using talk as a tool for learning.

Might this be a topic for a wider action research project?

Do you know of any other practitioners or professional associations who might like to hear about these materials, perhaps in your school cluster? We hope to continue to expand the Resource Bank in future; did your experience produce any resources or ideas that you would like to share with other teachers elsewhere? If the answer is 'yes' to either of these questions please email us via sch30@cam.ac.uk.

2.9 Further resources

References

Alexander, R.J. (2008) *Towards Dialogic Teaching. Rethinking Classroom Talk,* 4th edn. Cambridge: Dialogos UK Ltd.

Flitton, L. and Warwick, P. (2013) From classroom analysis to whole school professional development: promoting talk as a tool for learning across school departments, *Professional Development in Education*, 39(1): 99–121.

Littleton, K. and Howe, C. (2010) *Educational Dialogues: Understanding and Promoting Productive Interaction*. Abingdon: Routledge.

Mercer, N. (2000) *Words and Minds: How We Use Language to Think Together.* London: Routledge.

Mortimer, E.F. and Scott, P.H. (2003) *Meaning Making in Secondary Science Classrooms*. Milton Keynes: Open University Press.

All of the above books and reports are written in accessible language, provide examples from classroom practice in the UK and elsewhere, and are highly recommended for anyone wanting to read more about dialogue.

Web resources

See our own website at http://dialogueiwb.educ.cam.ac.uk/. This includes information about the underlying research and resulting publications and teachers' own case stories, together with their lesson materials and IWB flipcharts.

For more information about peer interaction within groups using the IWB themselves, see: http://iwbcollaboration.educ.cam.ac.uk/.

For considering the development of talk strategies in the classroom, go to: http://www.thinking-together.org.uk/.

An extensive review of the research into IWBs carried out in the UK and elsewhere is provided by Hennessy, S. and London, L. (2013) Learning from international experiences with interactive whiteboards: the role of professional development in integrating the technology, in OECD report *Review of the Italian Strategy for Digital Schools*. Paris: OECD Publishing. Available at: http://dx.doi.org/10.1787/5k487ntdbr44-en.

Note

1. Scaffolding refers to a teacher providing individualized support to facilitate a learner's development. It is assistance that helps the learner progress further than they could have done alone.

PART B

Reader

Note that all videos referred to in the Reader are available online at: http://tinyurl.com/OUPIWB

1 Creating a supportive environment for classroom dialogue

Simon Knight

Chapter summary

This chapter first considers the role of dialogue in classroom contexts, and the importance of open-ended dialogue in contrast to more traditional, closed questioning sequences. I briefly discuss the role of dialogue in individual psychological development, focusing on its importance for conceptual development in whole classes and small groups in the context of the classroom. A common – closed – sequence of classroom talk is first outlined, and then discussed in the context of 'dialogic talk' – talk which is more open, builds on prior knowledge, and is supportive and collaborative in nature. The use of 'exploratory talk' – talk which focuses on the use of reasoning to build mutual understanding – is also outlined in this context.

1. What role does dialogue play in learning?
2. What form does dialogue typically take?
3. How can we make dialogue more effective?

The second part of the chapter discusses some ways to promote effective dialogue in classroom contexts. Some suggestions for creating and identifying an effective environment for classroom talk are discussed. I highlight the importance of 'ground rules' for talk, and some key words teachers might look for and emphasize in encouraging the use of 'exploratory talk'. I then discuss some ideas for ways to start effective talk in classrooms, including the use of Talking Points and effective questioning. This chapter aims to give some background on effective dialogue of relevance to subsequent chapters, which will consider particular features of the IWB in the context of dialogue.

What place does dialogue have in the classroom? The importance of dialogue in classroom contexts

The Russian psychologist, Lev Vygotsky, highlighted the importance of language, emphasizing that:

> [W]hat children gain from their 'intermental' experience (communication between minds through social interaction) shapes their 'intramental' activity (the ways they think as individuals).

> What is more, he suggested that some of the most important influences on the development of thinking will come from the interaction between a learner and more knowledgeable, supportive members of their community. (Mercer 2003)

This highlights the significance of dialogue in learning. Wherever education is taking place, commonality – a shared perspective – is key, and dialogue is the tool used to create such a perspective (Edwards and Mercer 1987). Furthermore, the dialogue used to create 'common knowledge' is related to the educational development of children. Indeed, the strong consensus is that high-quality dialogue is associated with learning (see the collection edited by Littleton and Howe 2010). Engaging children in extended talk which encourages them to 'interthink' and explain themselves – as in the Thinking Together approach (Dawes et al. 2004) described below – stimulates both their subject learning, and general reasoning skills (Mercer et al. 1999; 2004; Mercer and Sams 2006; Rojas-Drummond et al. 2010), as well as their social and language skills (Wegerif et al. 2004).

With respect to direct pedagogical functions (as opposed to social functions such as behaviour management), dialogue seems to serve several purposes:

1. supporting individuals' subject learning
2. supporting psychological development – the development of oral language and reasoning skills
3. promoting whole-class and small-group understanding or commonality
4. enabling sharing of ideas that can be improved together (both whole class and small group) – a purpose the IWB is particularly well placed to serve, as later readings discuss.

A common classroom sequence

Classroom talk is typically rather different to ordinary conversation. It tends to focus on an individual, and for the majority of the time this individual is the teacher. Furthermore, there is a rather unequal balance in classroom communication, with particular rights, and expectations – including the expectation to confer or affirm 'correct' answers – placed on the teacher. Teachers commonly use talk to assess understanding, both of classes and individuals – indeed dialogue is essential in this pursuit. It is perhaps for this reason that a particular sort of exchange was noted by Sinclair and Coulthard (1975) as being especially common, the Initiation–Response–Feedback (IRF) exchange:

Initiation (by teacher) – What is the smallest prime number?
Response (by student) – 2
Feedback (by teacher) – Yes, well done.

Although these sequences provide easy means for assessment, there is a temptation not to explore beyond the individual student's answer (whether correct or incorrect), nor the reasoning and further understanding behind it (for example, why 2 might be an interesting prime).

Moving beyond questioning[1]

While the prevalence of this sequence has led to debate regarding its classroom use, such debates often fail to acknowledge two key points. First, that the IRF's prevalence may in part be attributed to the important – non-pedagogic – role of the classroom teacher in orchestrating classroom activity, assessing student performance, and relating such activities to the wider school accountability systems. Second, there has been an assumption that all IRF sequences perform the same function. Thus various sorts of questions ('can you pass the salt?', 'what is xyz?', 'do you think this is acceptable behaviour?') are treated in the same way. Yet it is clear that teachers' questions have a variety of intentions and communicative functions behind them – from classroom management, to seeking elaboration and, of course, assessing factual responses.

Dialogic talk and whole-class dialogue

Robin Alexander's (2001) research in the primary school classrooms of five countries has highlighted that, although dominance of classrooms by teacher talk is common, the types of contribution and the ways they are balanced vary. One factor in this variation was the length of response students gave to teacher questions; observations revealed some rather brief responses and other, longer, more reflective responses. The most effective of these interactions were conceptualized as being 'dialogic' in nature: 'Dialogic talk is that in which both teachers and students make substantial and significant contributions and through which students' thinking on a given idea or theme is helped to move forward. It may be used when teachers are interacting with groups or with whole classes' (Mercer 2003: 74).

Dialogic talk, then, is associated with the key benefits of dialogue described in the introduction. It enables both learners' intra- and intermental skills – their capacity to reason individually, and to engage with others in joint activity – and through this, their wider intellectual capabilities. Alexander (2008) summarizes the five key characteristics of dialogic education thus:

- **Collective:** teachers and children address learning tasks together, as a group or as a class, rather than in isolation
- **Reciprocal:** teachers and children listen to each other, share ideas and consider alternative viewpoints
- **Cumulative:** teachers and children build on their own and each other's ideas and chain them into coherent lines of thinking and enquiry
- **Supportive:** children articulate their ideas freely, without fear of embarrassment over 'wrong' answers and they help each other to reach common understandings
- **Purposeful:** teachers plan and facilitate dialogic teaching with particular educational goals in view.

Exploratory talk – a useful tool for effective dialogue

A related approach to thinking about dialogue which has been found useful builds on Mercer and colleagues' work on the Thinking Together project,[2] and Exploratory Talk. In this approach, 'group talk' is characterized as one of three 'types' – cumulative, disputational or exploratory (Mercer and Littleton 2007) as Table 1.1 indicates.

Table 1.1 Typology of talk

Type of talk	*Characteristics*	*Analysis*
Disputational	'Characterized by disagreement and individualized decision-making. There are few attempts to pool resources, to offer constructive criticism or make suggestions.'	'short exchanges, consisting of assertions and challenges or counter-assertions ("Yes it is. No it's not!").'
Cumulative	'Speakers build positively but uncritically on what the others have said. Partners use talk to construct "common knowledge" by accumulation.'	'Cumulative discourse is characterized by repetitions, confirmations and elaborations.'
Exploratory	'Partners engage critically but constructively with each other's ideas. Statements and suggestions are offered for joint consideration. These may be challenged and counter-challenged, but challenges are justified and alternative hypotheses are offered. Partners all actively participate, and opinions are sought and considered before decisions are jointly made. Compared with the other two types, in exploratory talk knowledge is made more publicly accountable and reasoning is more visible in the talk.'	Explanatory terms and phrases more common – for example, 'I think' 'because/'cause', 'if', 'for example', 'also'

Source: adapted from Mercer and Littleton (2007: 58–9).

These types of dialogue can be identified in whole-class and small-group activities. In whole-class exploratory talk, a dialogic approach to questioning is taken by the teacher, in which knowledge is built cumulatively, through the shared, guided, exploratory talk of the children. One such example was provided in the history lesson extract in the main resource in Section 2d (IWB Activity 3), and duplicated in Resource Appendix 4. Another example drawing directly on IWB use comes from whole-class dialogue captured during Diane Rawlins's second lesson on personal safety with 10- to 11-year-olds. In this example, groups are coming up to the IWB in turn and presenting outcomes of their group discussions ('as a team working for Childline') about a domestic violence scenario to the class; they write their suggestions next to the photographs they have selected and arranged from a set provided by Diane.

The teacher helped children to be responsive and build on each other's ideas through her open-ended, probing questions such as 'Why did Mehmet write "be assertive"?' 'Why are you [suggesting she calls the] police?' 'Does anyone agree that's a good step to take?' Her sensitive mediation spawned a number of thoughtful ideas, reasoned arguments and mature insights into the characters' mindsets as the class together explored some complex issues and ethical dilemmas (e.g. the worry that a family would be split up if a domestic violence situation was reported).

Video 15 shows this activity. Figure 1.1 captures one of the resulting IWB screens and it is followed by associated dialogue.

Image of 'divided loyalties' mask is reproduced by kind permission of the originator Wendy Morrell.

Figure 1.1 Representation of a small group's advice in a personal safety scenario

T (reading out what Courtney has written on the IWB): 'We must help you to inform the police.' Now why are you [suggesting she calls the] police? What is it about that information that made you think 'my advice is police'? Kalem.

Kalem (group member): Well we were thinking if we don't do anything it's just gonna keep on happening so we've got to do something about it. So we came up with an idea with calling the police.

T: And that would be some advice that you could give to that girl. Telling the girl she should call the police and tell them don't be afraid and tell them about what's happening to her friend Sam. That's a really big step isn't it. Does anybody agree that that's a good step to take? What do you think Rosie?

Rosie: I think that's good advice because if you inform the police then they could help, like in the future.

[. . .] Luke did you want to say something . . . Was there a piece of advice that your group thought was important?

Luke: If she's naughty, um, maybe that could be one of the reasons or if he's drinking too much or if he's a bit stressed, try not to go near him.

T: So some of those are the practical things, that's right. Did your group say anything about perhaps talking to a grown-up? Someone that you know, someone that you trust. Perhaps talking to somebody at school . . . Did your group say anything like that at all Shannon?

Shannon: Um, yeah . . . You could love (?) your family very much but try not to get too much involved because if you do and your(?) friend's dad might do . . .

T: Yeah, you see you're a child as well, aren't you, so maybe that's when you're saying that you'd go on and talk to adults. So what's Rosie [written]? 'Tell Sam go and get some help with the future and past bad things that have been happening.' Where do you think she might go for help? Where were you thinking when you wrote that?

Rosie: Like, the police and the family.

T: OK and Kalem is going to write something on behalf of her group. Did you want to say something?

Pupil: This is one of those ones that Rosie said, she said that these can help you for the future but if the police do arrest Sam's dad and if he gets out he can just hurt them more, if he gets near them.

T: Did you hear that? What do you think about that?

Jasmine: This is what you could do, you could have the police arrest your dad and sort of maybe give him some counselling, something's happened in the past that sort of made him violent or maybe sort of he has a drinking or drug problem.

T: So I suppose there is potential for something, might not necessarily be negative but it's not easy is it. My goodness it's a horribly difficult thing. And what have you written? 'Ask your mum is she allowed to sleep round more often'? And that's a way of perhaps saying, let me try and make something nice happen and maybe perhaps spend a bit more time around. I see some hands up . . . Go on then.

Kalem: But Sam says she doesn't want her family split up and if her dad gets arrested then they will split up.

T: Are you saying then that we should say and do nothing?

Kalem: We should do something but . . .

T: Also it's not our decision anyway is it? It's not our decision on what happens to Sam's dad but it is our decision about whether we do something. So generally then as a team of people working for Childline would you be telling Sam to or telling the friend rather. Tell Sam to contact somebody else, to tell somebody else. We're giving information like that. We're saying to be assertive and that it might get serious. Oh, this was a tough one wasn't it?

The Thinking Together[3] website based at the University of Cambridge gives some typical sequences of each talk type (Mercer 2008) in small-group work. The sequence below, between Elenor, Georgie and Carmel discussing the truth of a statement on 'Our galaxy', is taken from that site and indicates some of the characteristics we find in 'exploratory talk' episodes.

Elenor: OK (reads) 'The moon changes shape because it is in the shadow of the earth'.

Carmel: No, that's not true, because there's the clouds that cover the moon.

Elenor: No it isn't . . . yeah.

Georgie: Yeah.

Elenor: Because in the day we think 'oh the moon's gone'; it hasn't gone, it's just the cloud that . . .

Carmel: . . . have covered it.

Georgie: Yeah, that's why I like, every time, well on Sunday I went out and it was like five in the morning right, and the moon was still out so that's fine 'cos it was still dark, right.

Elenor: Yeah.

Georgie: So when we went out it was like five, four, four o'clock, something like that, like at that time there wouldn't be the moon out would there, but I saw half the moon out and I said, I said to my mum's friend, I said look Tony, there's the moon already out, and he said oh yeah. 'Cos in the morning, when we came there was the clouds.

Teacher: OK everybody, finish up the one you're talking about.

Elenor: So what do we think?

Georgie: I think it's false.

Carmel: False.

It is important to note that often dialogue will contain elements of each type of talk, and indeed that there are times when one type of talk might be more appropriate than another. However, higher levels of exploratory talk are associated with the educational gains discussed in the introduction to this chapter. A typical pattern of research in these studies has involved an intervention including the development of classroom 'ground rules for exploratory talk', followed by lessons which are specifically designed to encourage high-quality dialogic talk which engages learners in reasoning, and explaining their ideas to one another. The typology provides teachers with a simple way to understand the nature of the talk in their own classrooms, and – through encouraging explanation, elaboration and mutual listening – can provide some clear ways to improve the quality of classroom talk, as will now be outlined further.

Promoting effective dialogue

Ground rules

In setting up effective dialogue, the prior experiences and expectations of the children should be considered. In order for pupils to engage effectively in whole-class and small-group dialogue, some rules should be established. These are best derived from children's own awareness of what makes a good discussion. Their own experience of group work can help children to suggest the framework which will promote exploratory talk if adhered to by all; active listening, a level of challenge, the giving and asking for of reasons, and an inclusive ethos. When introducing students to the class ground rules for exploratory talk teachers can elicit rules that will generate exploratory talk, discuss them in some more depth, and then refer back to them for example using a printed poster or a scrolling heading on the IWB, in subsequent lessons. The IWB affords some opportunity to discuss and annotate such ground rules, and then return to them at a later date if it is felt that they should be amended. You may find the resources on the Thinking Together website[4] (Dawes 2008a) useful for this purpose. The Thinking Together materials[5] (Thinking Together Group n.d.) suggest the following as some basic ground rules for constructive dialogue (the web page itself also provides a student-friendly version):

Our class ground rules for exploratory talk:

- everyone in the group is encouraged to contribute
- contributions are treated with respect
- reasons are asked for
- everyone is prepared to accept challenges

- alternatives are discussed before a decision is taken
- all relevant information is shared
- the group seeks to reach agreement.

Exploratory talk

These ground rules should help to guide students to avoid unconstructive criticism, while seeking well-founded reasoning in their dialogue. In addition to these ground rules, teachers should think about the types of talk they model, including in their explanations of key ideas. Although far from an exhaustive list, some key words associated with exploratory talk are:

Think	listen	exploratory talk	discuss	agree	disagree
reason	opinion	because	if	why	knowledge
information	negotiate	compromise	decide	joint	team
collaborate	group	question	active listening		a good
point/idea/reason		changed my mind	learned		I don't follow
I don't understand		please say more/explain/elaborate			sum up
present		clear description	articulate		fluent

(Dawes 2012)

Encouraging the use of these key words, providing prompts for their use, and ensuring enough time to engage appropriately with constructive dialogue are crucial for developing educationally effective talk skills. In addition, teachers should consider the particular skills and purposes for which students engage in dialogue and their use of Talk for Learning – which should give opportunities to explore:

1. How and why to include all group members in a discussion
2. How to attend, listen, reflect and hold thoughts in mind, taking turns in a discussion
3. How to ask for and give reasons, and to evaluate and discuss the basis for reasons
4. How to elaborate and explain, keeping a focus on the topic under discussion
5. How to summarize key ideas and negotiate an agreement. (Dawes 2012)[6]

Teachers should also consider the opportunities they provide for such talk, its sequencing, and the use of effective prompts for talk which could include artefacts, and the use of Talking Points.

Talking Points (adapted from Dawes 2012)

Talking Points provide prompts for students to discuss key concepts, areas to explore or misconceptions. They are designed specifically to encourage debate and talk that puts children in the position of having to justify their ideas and articulate their thinking. Teachers may find it useful to write Talking Points as part of their sequence of lessons, which flag up the key concepts and potential misconceptions for students to discuss. They are not questions, but rather statements which might be considered 'true, false or unsure' – statements which can be rationally considered. For example, you could consider with some colleagues whether you think the Talking Points below are true, false or neither, and then consider how these points relate to the curriculum talking points underneath, and your own teaching:

Professional development Talking Points
- Group work **should** finish in one lesson.
- Groups should be formed with the **same** students every time.
- Group work should **always promote** competition amongst different groups.

Curriculum Talking Points
- Things stop when they run out of force.
- Things that give out light (like the sun) are always hot.
- Dark is a form of energy that is weaker than light.
- Poor people are lazy.
- Some people, like footballers, get paid too much.
- You cannot throw things away, because there is no such place as 'away'.

As Dawes (2008b) describes,[7] Talking Points provide one way to develop the skills highlighted above, and can serve as a useful way to remind children of ideas they have previously encountered. Indeed, particularly on this latter point, the IWB might be a useful way to explore Talking Points, which may be annotated, linked back to previous work, or associated with other artefacts such as diagrams. These might also provide a useful starting point for some higher-order thinking in asking students to think of their own Talking Points. In this sort of exercise teachers should consider their usual pedagogic decisions regarding tasks, and group allocation, in relation to – not separation from – their thinking regarding the types and topics of talk they would like the students to engage in.

Effective use of questioning in whole-class dialogue

Resources that stimulate and sustain group talk can be thought of as one part of a dialogic classroom in which questioning goes beyond a typical IRF exchange of closed questions and factual responses, and towards a classroom which engages in open-ended questioning – a dialogic, questioning classroom. Much has been made of the value of high-quality questioning, and it is not our intention to rehash these debates here, except to highlight the synergy between those discussions and our own. In particular, we note that Bloom's taxonomy is often found to be a useful tool in thinking about one's questioning. The research presented here provides further support for the claim that teachers should seek to move away from the lowest – closed, factual recall – questions, and towards more advanced questioning. This shift should bear in mind that the aim is not necessarily to ask a question, and receive a concise answer; but rather to engage in a sequence of dialogic, exploratory questioning, which develops understanding through the language it uses – through sustained interthinking.

While the typical IRF sequence is between teacher and student, the dialogic classroom should be more open to *student–student* and *student–teacher* questioning. This is particularly interesting in the context of the IWB given the affordances of that tool towards recording, structuring and linking ideas over time in a mutually supportive environment, while developing understanding of the idea's relationships, how they support or contest each other and how they may be built upon. It is to this topic that subsequent chapters turn.

Conclusions: recognizing high-quality dialogue

Both exploratory talk and dialogic talk:

- Build ideas, constructively, acknowledging what has been said before
- Are not monopolized by individuals (including the teacher) but are inclusive and open for contribution
- Respect the contributions of others
- Involve reasoning together, and sometimes the use of thinking aloud – interthinking – to develop understanding
- Are 'open-ended', encouraging hypothesis, questioning, challenge, elaboration and negotiation, rather than 'closed' involving the citing of only one 'correct' answer
- Can be planned for by teachers who have considered the concepts they are tackling, the time that will be needed and the skills that students will need to talk constructively.

Group talk – whether whole class or small group – requires time to be effective. Planning should reflect this requirement, and the need for students to understand the sequencing of their learning. 'Classroom learning . . . depends on learners having some understanding of how and why tasks are designed and ordered as they are . . . . Dialogue is the medium: dialogue about activity that has yet to start, that is on-going, and that has been brought to a close' (Blanchard 2008: 145).

For students to fully engage in dialogue, teachers should consider the sequence of concepts they are tackling, and the potential misconceptions that learners might encounter. The use of Talking Points and other Talk for Learning strategies in a mutually supportive environment that makes explicit and respects the ground rules for exploratory talk is crucial if every pupil is to benefit from dialogue.

Acknowledgements

Many thanks to Lyn Dawes for her contribution of resources and useful comments on an earlier draft of this chapter.

Notes

1. This and the next section are adapted from Mercer (2003); direct quotations are indicated as such where included. The whole article can be read at http://tinyurl.com/Mercer2003; sections from that article are also adapted and used across the wiki.
2. http://www.thinking-together.org.uk.
3. http://www.thinking-together.org.uk.
4. http://tinyurl.com/usefulrules1.
5. http://tinyurl.com/groundrules1.
6. See also Dawes and Mercer (2008) at: http://tinyurl.com/DawesMercer.
7. See also chapter pre-print on the Thinking Together website at: http://tinyurl.com/Dawes2008.

References

Alexander, R. (2001) *Culture and Pedagogy: International Comparisons in Primary Education*. Oxford: Wiley.

Alexander, R. (2008) *Towards Dialogic Teaching: Rethinking Classroom Talk,* 4th edn. Cambridge: Dialogos.

Blanchard, J. (2008) Learning awareness: constructing formative assessment in the classroom, in the school and across schools. *Curriculum Journal*, 19(3): 137. doi:10.1080/09585170802357454.

Dawes, L. (2008a) Are these useful rules for discussion? Thinking Together Resources, University of Cambridge. Available at: http://thinkingtogether.educ.cam.ac.uk/resources/Are_these_useful_rules_for_discussion.pdf [Accessed 21 May 2013].

Dawes, L. (2008b) *The Essential Speaking and Listening*. Abingdon: David Fulton.

Dawes, L. (2012) *Talking Points: Discussion Activities in the Primary Classroom*. Abingdon: Routledge.

Dawes, L. and Mercer, N. (2008) Talking points; what does your group think about these ideas? Thinking Together Resources, University of Cambridge. Available at: http://thinkingtogether.educ.cam.ac.uk/resources/Talking_points_about_group_talk.pdf [Accessed 21 May 2013].

Dawes, L., Mercer, N. and Wegerif, R. (2004) *Thinking Together: A Programme of Activities for Developing Speaking, Listening and Thinking Skills for Children Aged 8–11*. Birmingham: Imaginative Minds.

Edwards, D. and Mercer, N. (1987) *Common Knowledge: The Development of Understanding in the Classroom*. London: Routledge.

Littleton, K. and Howe, C. (2010) *Educational Dialogues: Understanding and Promoting Productive Interaction*. Abingdon: Routledge.

Mercer, N. (2003) The educational value of dialogic talk in whole-class dialogue. *New Perspectives on Spoken English in the Classroom. English. 2003: discussion papers* (pp. 73–6). Qualifications and Curriculum Authority. Available at: http://rose.bristol.ac.uk/handle/1983/1004 [Accessed 21 May 2013].

Mercer, N. (2008) Three kinds of talk. Thinking Together Resources, University of Cambridge. Available at: http://thinkingtogether.educ.cam.ac.uk/resources/5_examples_of_talk_in_groups.pdf [Accessed 21 May 2013].

Mercer, N. and Littleton, K. (2007) *Dialogue and the Development of Children's Thinking: A Sociocultural Approach,* new edn. Abingdon: Routledge.

Mercer, N. and Sams, C. (2006) Teaching children how to use language to solve maths problems, *Language and Education*, 20(6): 507–28.

Mercer, N., Dawes, L., Wegerif, R. and Sams, C. (2004) Reasoning as a scientist: ways of helping children to use language to learn science, *British Educational Research Journal*, 30(3): 359–77.

Mercer, N., Wegerif, R. and Dawes, L. (1999) Children's talk and the development of reasoning in the classroom. *British Educational Research Journal*, 25(1): 95–111. doi:10.1080/0141192990250107.

Rojas-Drummond, S., Littleton, K., Hernández, F. and Zúñiga, M. (2010) Dialogical interactions among peers in collaborative writing contexts, in K. Littleton and C. Howe (eds) *Educational Dialogues: Understanding and Promoting Productive Interaction*. Abingdon: Routledge.

Sinclair, J.M.H. and Coulthard, M. (1975) *Towards an Analysis of Discourse: The English Used by Teachers and Pupils*. Oxford: Oxford University Press.

Thinking Together Group (n.d.) Ground rules for exploratory talk. Thinking Together Resources, University of Cambridge. Available at: http://thinkingtogether.educ.cam.ac.uk/resources/Ground_rules_for_Exploratory_Talk.pdf [Accessed 21 May 2013].

Wegerif, R., Littleton, K., Dawes, L., Mercer, N. and Rowe, D. (2004) Widening access to educational opportunities through teaching children how to reason together, *Westminster Studies in Education*, 27(2): 143. doi:10.1080/0140672040270205.

2 Supporting dialogic teaching of personal safety with the interactive whiteboard in an urban primary school

Diane Rawlins

Chapter summary

This case study examined how use of interactive whiteboards (IWBs) could support a 'dialogic teaching' approach to the learning of Personal, Social, Health and Citizenship Education (PSHCE). The work explored how interactive and multimodal features of the whiteboard can be exploited to allow learners to manipulate a wide range of resources in the course of expressing and developing ideas together. The study developed and trialled a series of three lessons on Personal Safety carried out with Year 6 students (aged 10–11). The lessons were planned after a series of project workshops stimulating three teacher participants to reflect on and develop our own practice, to debate illustrated approaches, and to work collaboratively with university researchers in developing a shared view of both classroom 'dialogue' and strategies for using the IWB to support it. Lessons were videoed, teacher participants were interviewed three times and kept diaries, and collaborative video analyses characterized the strategies used.

In my own study, I was particularly interested to explore how I could help our staff to develop use of the IWB to support a dialogic approach in our classrooms. Further evidence here was gathered through analysing the impact of the lesson filming, interviewing and workshop discussions on my own practice, particularly towards developing our group's 'dialogue table' to make it accessible and useful to teachers. The main findings of the study were that using the IWB can make a significant contribution to developing a dialogic approach, but that there are a number of factors which must be addressed in order to maximize the effectiveness of what teachers do; for example, IWB skill level, an understanding of the dialogic approach, and being (or becoming) a reflective and adaptive practitioner.

Introduction and focus of the study

Interactive whiteboards have become common in primary classrooms. As a senior teacher (Deputy Head) in my school, I visit and observe lessons regularly, and I see teachers using the IWB in different ways to stimulate, record and frame lessons. I was interested to put this practical, school-based experience alongside the views and perspectives of the members of our group as we explored our understanding of Dialogic Teaching (DT) and particularly of the potential of the IWB to support DT in our classrooms, with a view to supporting professional development of our staff in the future.

Workshop days were extremely helpful in providing space, time, resources and input from colleagues which would allow me to reflect on how my own practice could be developed further, and led me to decide on this focus for my research: what are the key factors which will allow primary teachers to fully exploit the IWB to aid the development of a dialogic approach to teaching and learning?

Context for the study

Arbury Primary School is a two-form entry primary school in an urban setting in Cambridge, with approximately 350 children on roll from Reception to Year 6. The school serves a mixed catchment of families in council- and privately-owned housing, with around 21 per cent of families eligible for Free School Meals. Around 30 per cent of our children are on our Special Needs Register, and 24 per cent have English as a second or additional language. Teachers are skilled at meeting the children's very diverse needs, and the school's contextual data indicates that by Year 6 most children are achieving at, or above, the national average.

Teaching plan

My class of 25 Year 6 children formed a diverse group, with a significant number presenting challenging behaviour and with social and emotional difficulties. I was setting clear expectations of behaviour and attitude towards learning, and trying to include a range of teaching and learning styles that would engage and motivate learners.

The first three lessons in a half term scheme of work on 'Personal Safety' within the PSHCE Scheme of Work were filmed. These lessons were based on guidance by the Cambridgeshire 'Staying Safe' Scheme, produced by the Education Child Protection Unit (Theme 4: Secrets, Promises and Tricks).

Dialogue always plays a significant role in my teaching style: observers have commented on my 'conversational' style of teaching; but with the content of these Personal Safety lessons, it was especially important that the children were able to talk with focus about issues and opinions, to begin to articulate why particular safety rules are important. I was also consciously trying not to reiterate or reformulate children's contributions, but encouraging children to question each other.

We have IWBs in all our classrooms; I have been using my Promethean board for nearly five years. The IWB is very much a central part of our lessons, being used in many different ways. However, being involved in the project workshop days had given me many ideas about how I might integrate the IWB into my lessons in new ways. For example, the practical guidance from the IWB-expert teacher gave me confidence and practical skills to use video clips and sound recording as part of the lesson. Additionally, having some input on using software features, such as layering, to make short, interactive games and activities, opened up many possible choices for me. In fact, it was important to rein in the impulse to include too many 'tricks'! Table 2.1 (overleaf) summarizes the content of the three lessons I planned and Appendix B2.1 (at http://tinyurl.com/OUPIWB) contains the ActivPrimary flipcharts I prepared for them.

Research plan

The research plan allowed me to learn more about both the IWB and dialogic teaching, and to develop at a rate that was challenging but supportive. It was conducted in three phases, as outlined below. (Further information about the methodology of the joint video review, and how this worked in my own case in particular, can be seen in a couple of published articles: Hennessy et al. 2011 and Warwick et al. 2011.)

Phase 1

Professional development activity

I participated in three whole team one-day workshops that employed various resources as stimuli for reflecting on my own practice. Together, we evaluated the illustrated approaches and assessed their applicability to our own contexts. We discussed ways of further exploiting the IWB technology to enhance our own approaches to dialogic interaction and worked on refining our notions of 'dialogue'.

Table 2.1 Overview of personal safety lesson sequence

	Content	*DT opportunities*	*PD link*	*IWB use*
Lesson 1	Explored the ideas behind secrets, when do we keep a secret and loyalty in relation to keeping friend's secrets. (See video clip at http://sms.cam.ac.uk/media/1097541)	Opportunities for whole-class and group talk	Consideration of how to prompt dialogue influenced IWB use	IWB used as a starter with images and a ticker-tape message. Children had previously recorded views on secrets onto the IWB to discuss them in the lesson.
Lesson 2	Explored what action to take when a friend shares a secret. (See video clips at http://sms.cam.ac.uk/media/1098026, http://sms.cam.ac.uk/media/1085308	Opportunities to explore use of a Teaching Assistant as a recorder of pupil ideas, and use of 'ground rules' to support talk (see Chapter 1 by Knight)	Considerations of dialogic *process* as more important or as important as content outcomes prompted this lesson	Children gave advice on a problem which was displayed and read out from the IWB, with a recording re-played throughout the lesson, and images added to those used in previous lessons
Lesson 3	Applying knowledge of decision making in personal safety to justify judgements about what action to take	Opportunity to use self-selected groups and flipcharts from the three lessons	Two TAs supported the lesson and some task differentiation and thus additional planning was required	Collected final DVD evidence and used images and annotations accumulated over lesson series

Resources and data

I kept unstructured diary notes of my reflections on pilot lessons and workshop experiences. We received input during the workshops both from an IWB-experienced expert teacher and from academic members of the team, which included professional development activities generated by prior 'Thinking Together' research on the development of children's language and reasoning in the classroom (Mercer and Littleton 2007), plus video footage from the T-MEDIA interactive CD-ROMs (http://t-media.educ.cam.ac.uk/). Copies of Alexander's (2004) treatise on Dialogic Teaching, a chapter on interactive versus non-interactive and dialogic versus authoritative communication approaches (Mortimer and Scott 2003), and a short article on questioning strategies (Cardellichio and Field 1997) were also distributed.

Classroom implications and activity

At this early stage, I found the specific input on the work of Robin Alexander and Neil Mercer very interesting, as it resonated with the work we have been doing in school on Assessment for Learning, developing teachers' questioning skills and developing Speaking and Listening. It also confirmed that teachers must create a secure setting in their class, forming strong working relationships with children; I noted this particularly after watching the initial video recordings. At this point in the research, I began to feel that my focus should be on how teachers use a range of techniques and strategies, including creative and effective use of the IWB to foster the conditions in their classrooms within which dialogic teaching can thrive, leading to more engaged learners.

Phase 2

Professional development activity

A sequence of three lessons was videoed in my classroom. I continued to keep diary notes outlining my pre- and post-lesson reflections and planning. I spent a day in school working alongside our ICT Co-ordinator to look at the kind of flipcharts being used in lessons and which new IWB features we would share at a staff meeting.

Resources and data

I was interviewed once about my plans and again after each lesson. Additional data, such as flipchart files (including captured annotations), lesson plans, children's informal annotations, digital photographs and copies of student work were collected to support understanding of the context of the class and the lessons.

Classroom implications and activity

We looked at example flipcharts on our network, being interested in the use of images, whether flipcharts were being made simply as a lesson 'script', or whether they had the possibility of being used flexibly as an ongoing record/stimulus/means of review. On a practical level, we arranged for all teachers to have the latest version of ActivPrimary software and the resources updated and installed.

Phase 3

Professional development activity

Our IWB/Dialogic Teaching staff meeting was conducted with the ICT Co-ordinator and project researchers. It involved a basic introduction to Dialogic Teaching and some new IWB features: a 'make a copy' function, new to the most recent version of ActivPrimary; and using the transparency facility to layer images/text on a flipchart page. Teachers then had time (and support) during the meeting to make a flipchart page using these new features. They were well motivated, with a number expressing the view that there is never enough time to learn and try out new features!

Resources and data

Although I did not undertake any formal response gathering, I did observe a trainee teacher the following day using the transparency facility, comparing images of a classroom in Ghana and one of the classrooms she was based in. The Year 2 children were very engaged by being able to compare the two classrooms in this slightly different way, and were suggesting many appropriate similarities and differences. Having observed the trainee teaching the previous week, I noted a much more sophisticated level of oral responses from the children in this lesson.

In our research group, copies of the lesson videos were distributed during this phase and the whole team met again for a fourth half-day workshop to review our experiences and continue our evolving construction of dialogue.

Classroom implications and activity

The analysis enabled us to identify what our data revealed about the integration of IWB use to support substantive teacher–student and student–student dialogues. The newly developed teaching approaches were scrutinized, debated and refined.

Research findings

What are the key factors which will allow primary teachers to fully exploit the IWB to aid the development of a dialogic approach to teaching and learning?

In this section, I outline the three factors which I believe to have been the most influential in leading to the development of a more dialogic approach in my own teaching, and which have the potential to do the same for other primary teachers.

1. Creating the conditions for dialogue to thrive

The key elements of this factor are that the classroom practice is founded on high-quality teaching approaches and teacher skill, and includes a commitment to flexible, adaptive, responsive, inclusive teaching.

(i) Understanding of dialogic teaching: *The teacher must have an understanding of what a dialogic approach involves and reflect on how it relates to current classroom practice.*

The research team's work on dialogic teaching resulted in continual changes and reviews of our dialogic table in light of discussion about what dialogue should 'look like', the conditions for learning, the strategies, activities, approaches and outcomes we might see. This table was briefly shared with staff at our IWB/DT staff meeting. On behalf of the research team I first developed it further to make it more 'teacher-friendly' (see the resulting Dialogue Table in Resource Appendix 2), changing the original headings and subsequently adding in some practical guidance (see bold font in Expanded Dialogue Table in Resource Appendix 3).

(ii) Being responsive to children's level of involvement in lessons: *The teacher should notice and respond to children's engagement with tasks and reflect this in adapted planning or changes mid-lesson if appropriate.*

An example which illustrates this well, comes from the first lesson of the series, in which Melissa volunteered to take charge of her group, which was something I would not have anticipated, as she was usually very passive and reserved in whole-class situations. The fact that she felt confident enough to have a go at leading a group indicated to me that she felt supported and comfortable with this form of learning. This reminded me that we must be open and responsive to the different ways in which children respond to different teaching and learning styles.

(iii) Teachers should be well informed and skilled in order to support children with particular needs: *Some children will require input during lessons to enable them to participate as fully as possible.*

During Lesson 3, a child with ADHD [attention deficit hyperactivity disorder] was keen to explain his understanding of one of our scenarios, but began to outline an unsafe method of dealing with the tricky situation. I intervened at this time to help him understand the potentially dangerous solution he was suggesting; it was important to do this in a way which helped him to still feel positive about his contributions, but also to help everyone to realize that there are some basic safety rules we should never break.

2. Supporting children in accessing learning through dialogue

Success in this area seemed to be supported by teacher skill in selecting appropriate resources and implementing ways of working which nurture a dialogic way of learning, including:

(i) Careful selection of images which can be used over a series of lessons and may come to represent a concept or discussion around the subject: e.g. the image of two girls, where one is whispering to the other, came to represent our discussion about secrets; images could be used to gather ideas or to help summarize opinions.

(ii) Talk rules (see Chapter 1 by Knight and **Videos 1 and 2**): giving explicit guidance on talk and how we can work together on talk-based tasks is important, so that all children understand their role in the learning. The rules also reassure children, provided they are backed up by good-quality practice in the classroom, that their input is valued and valuable in our learning.

(iii) Planning should include opportunities for talk which are not just focused on getting the 'right answer', but may involve speculating, questioning, criticizing and building new understandings of concepts. This must be backed up by skilled teacher intervention in modelling and prompting children to question each other's ideas and views, e.g. 'X, what do you think about Y's idea?'

3. Exploring the potential for employing the IWB as a dialogic teaching tool

This factor again has some practical issues, which have to be addressed in order for teachers to make full use of the IWB in supporting dialogue in the classroom.

(i) Access to support, inspirational ideas and time to experiment are all key issues. Our meetings with colleagues and the ICT Co-ordinator were useful for understanding and seeing examples of IWB features, and gave teachers time to experiment with these features.

(ii) Planning should also be flexible and designed to try out features in a way which will allow them to be used in a creative and open-ended way: sound-recording is a good example of a very simple technique which worked most effectively in a couple of different ways. I recorded myself reading a text to be used in the second lesson, and I was able to observe the children's reactions whilst they were hearing the text for the first time. I could not have done this had I been reading the text to them. Additionally, children were very motivated by recording their own views straight onto the flipchart pages; it is very simple to do, and they can revisit earlier views by listening to them again, potentially noting where their thinking has changed as a result of subsequent learning.

(iii) Point ii highlights the need for opportunities for children to see the IWB as not just the teacher's resource, but their own; a resource which can aid them in recording or presenting their views.

Conclusions and recommendations

- Evidence from the lesson observations indicates that IWB use and the dialogic approach have impact on children's participation in lessons and on their learning in different ways; but that for this to happen, the classroom climate must encourage and support inclusion.
- Staff need a shared understanding of what dialogue in the classroom looks like; my version of the Expanded Dialogue Table (Resource Appendix 3), annotated with guidance and ideas from team discussions, could be a useful way of ensuring this happens. Teaching Assistants also need to be a part of this understanding, so that they can support the dialogic approach effectively.
- Practical support is needed to encourage experimentation and creativity towards confidently using the multimodal features of the IWB in lessons.
- Practical issues to be considered include allowing time to gather images when planning a topic or series of lessons; making sure lesson planning is creative and not formulaic, and includes a range of teaching and learning opportunities.
- Building in time to review and reflect: how do we know whether dialogue is happening? Teachers may also wish to monitor themselves or be observed with this as a specific focus, perhaps using the Dialogue Table (Resource Appendix 2) as a 'tick list'.

One of the 'big questions' raised by these conclusions and recommendations is 'could the dialogue table become the guidance in your school policy for teaching and learning?' See the whole-school Action Plan (Resource Appendix 9) I produced for my own school that may be of interest.

Evaluation and reflection

For my learning to be truly worthwhile, it must be shared, and I now look forward to carrying out professional development work with our staff, who are committed to providing the best teaching that we can. This opportunity to work on a different plane from my usual, practical-based approach was illuminating in many ways, and I found it refreshing to be working collaboratively to develop definitions of how dialogue would 'look' in our classrooms, and to pinpoint how and for what purposes the IWB was actually being used within a lesson.

At Arbury, we are involved in working closely with the Faculty's Primary PGCE trainees and within the county with newly qualified teachers on developing behaviour management strategies. I can see many opportunities for sharing my enhanced understanding of how to create the conditions for dialogue to thrive, and how to support it by employing the interactive features of the IWB.

Acknowledgements

Many thanks to Simon Knight for his careful editing of this chapter, and to all the children who participated in the study in my school.

References

Alexander, R.J. (2004) *Towards Dialogic Teaching. Rethinking Classroom Talk.* Cambridge: Dialogos.

Cardellichio, T. and Field, W. (1997) Seven strategies that encourage neural branching, *Educational Leadership,* 54(6): 33–6.

Hennessy, S., Warwick, P. and Mercer, N. (2011) A dialogic inquiry approach to working with teachers in developing classroom dialogue, *Teachers College Record,* 113(9): 1906–59. Available at: http://tinyurl.com/TCR2011. [Accessed 21 May 2013].

Mercer, N. and Littleton, K. (2007) *Dialogue and the Development of Children's Thinking.* London: Routledge.

Mortimer, E.F. and Scott, P.H. (2003) *Meaning Making in Secondary Science Classrooms*. Milton Keynes: Open University Press.

Warwick, P., Hennessy, S. and Mercer, N. (2011) Promoting teaching and school development through co-enquiry: developing interactive whiteboard use in a 'dialogic classroom', *Teachers and Teaching: Theory and Practice*, 17(3): 303–24. doi:10.1080/13540602.2011.554704.

Appendices

(Electronic versions only, available at http://tinyurl.com/OUPIWB)

B2.1 Flipchart pages from Diane's Lesson 1
B2.2 Flipchart pages from Diane's Lesson 2
B2.3 Flipchart pages from Diane's Lesson 3

3 Developing a dialogic approach to interactive whiteboard use in English: teacher reflections and student perceptions

Caroline Neale

Chapter summary

My small-scale case study explored how interactive whiteboards (IWBs) can be used to support dialogic teaching in English in a middle school. Through exploiting the interactive and multimodal features of the interactive whiteboard, my students were encouraged to express and develop their ideas through collaborative interaction at and around the IWB. In the study, I developed and trialled a series of three lessons on crime writing with my Year 8 students (aged 12–13) which are reported in this chapter. These lessons were planned following a series of workshops involving teachers and university researchers: we worked together to establish a shared understanding of what dialogic teaching is and to initiate strategies for using the IWB to facilitate this approach (further details about the research and workshops are presented in Chapter 2). My study included a focus on students' perceptions of the use of the IWB as a classroom resource and their views on talk as a tool for learning. Opinions were gathered through a student questionnaire. Key findings include:

- The majority of students stated that they preferred lessons where the IWB was used as a tool for supporting dialogic teaching and learning.
- Students were able to give specific examples of how the IWB enhanced their learning in the classroom.
- Interestingly, students preferred working in friendship groups and more productive talk was stimulated in these groupings than in teacher-selected groups.

Introduction and focus of the study

In workshop discussions at the start of the project, it was established that, in the view of teacher participants and the research team, the potential strength of IWB technology lay in its support for expressing and testing learners' ideas, and collaboratively constructing new knowledge. The IWB's *interactivity* and *multimodality* offer rapid manipulation of text, colour and shape, plus sound, static and moving images. The tool may therefore provide new opportunities for learners to express and reformulate ideas in verbal and visual forms, as elaborated in Chapter 5.

As an English teacher, I teach Speaking and Listening skills explicitly (Attainment Target 1 in the English National Curriculum), and I am fully aware of, and committed to, the importance of talk as a tool for learning. My classes were used to engaging in whole-class discussions and using allocated roles such as chairperson, spokesperson, scribe and so on (Mercer 1995). Taking part in the workshops at the outset of the project enabled me to look more closely at what constitutes effective dialogue within a classroom, and to identify areas I wanted to develop further. I was already using the IWB in almost every lesson: however, I had not considered how I could explicitly use it to support talk. I was also interested to find out whether the students shared my views about the value of the IWB and of dialogue. The study therefore addressed three research questions, one exploring my perspective as a teacher and the others focusing on students' perspectives:

- How can I, as a teacher with a firmly established dialogic approach, exploit the multimodality and interactivity of the IWB to support student learning?
- What value do students place on the use of the IWB and the use of talk in a classroom setting?
- What insights can students offer in order to help us further support their learning?

Context for the study

At the time I was a Leader of English and Drama/Media in a middle school in North Hertfordshire, with students aged 9 to 13 years (Years 5–8). There were 460 students on roll. My study was conducted during Spring and Summer terms 2008, with follow-up review meetings in Autumn 2008 (the following academic year). The students were a top set Year 8 English group (11 boys, 14 girls) who were generally a high-achieving, hard-working group: however, they were also a group characterized by their quietness and it was noticeable that boys dominated in responding to teacher-led questions. The seating plan was changed on a termly basis, and where possible, students were placed in a boy–girl pairing. The classroom was laid out in a 'table group' setting, with students sitting in 'within-group' mixed ability groups of between two and six. A new seating plan was put in place a week before the filming of the lessons, and it appeared that this resulted in students being even quieter than usual.

Teaching plan

Three lessons were devised to trial strategies focused on using key features of the IWB to support dialogue. These lessons formed part of a four-week Crime Writing unit, the aim of which was for students to produce an extended crime story, demonstrating an understanding of the genre.

Lesson 1

The lesson's aim was to use a real-life crime story, 'The Almost Perfect Murder' to allow students to become familiar with crime vocabulary and to develop their analysis, reasoning and justification skills. The opening activity (see Figure 3.1 and Slides 1–3 of the SMART Notebook file for Lesson 1 in Appendix B3.1) was designed for students to discuss possible scenarios arising from an abandoned briefcase and its contents. IWB slides (Slides 5 and 6 in Notebook file in Appendix B3.1) were created to initially provide a visual stimulus to accompany the text and then to present a task summary when students were working on comprehension questions. See **Video 16** of this activity.

The plenary for the lesson was the 'Badge of Truth' (see Figure 3.2) where students were asked to select a statement from the board, decide whether it was true or false, providing reasons for their view, and then move the statement into the 'Badge of Truth'. With prior formatting of the statements using Smart Notebook software, if the statement was true, it would remain in front of the badge, if it was false, it would 'magically' disappear behind it (see Resource Bank for instructions on how to create a 'magic box' of this kind).

Lesson 2

This lesson helped students to develop an understanding of crime scene clues. Students watched a short video clip showing an incompetent bank robber (downloaded from YouTube and imported into the

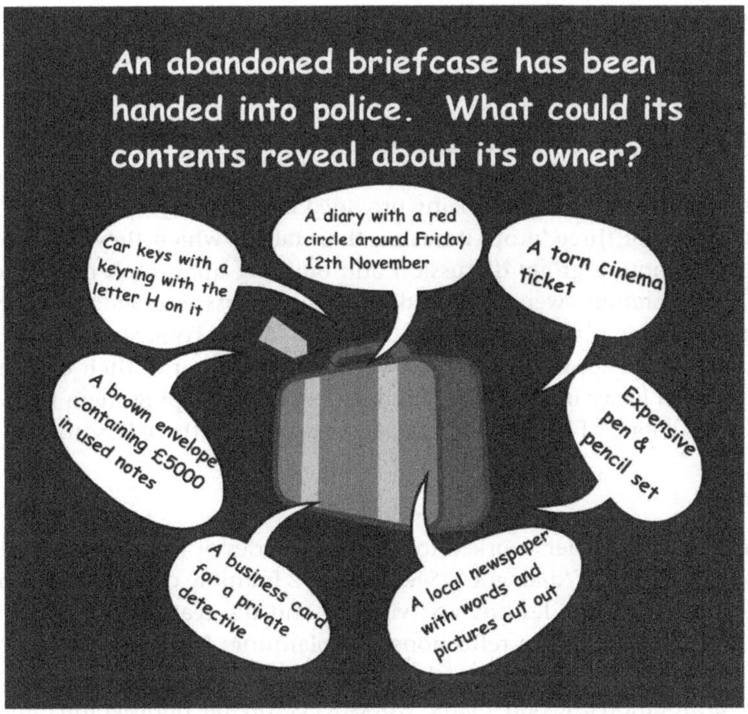

Figure 3.1 'Abandoned briefcase' scenario slide

Notebook software), followed by a Material Detectives clip from a Science Zone DVD where a house was broken into and clues left. These clips were used to stimulate discussion in table groups about the evidence left and how it might be investigated. Students were given a sketch of the crime scene and a series of multiple choice 'logic' questions linked to what they could see in the sketch and additional information displayed on the IWB (see Slide 4 for Lesson 2 in Notebook flipchart in Appendix B3.2). Working in pairs or groups to discuss the evidence, students had to decide who committed the crime. This task required students to make their thinking and reasoning explicit and gave them a shared purpose for their talk. The plenary task also used the IWB (see Slide 7 for Lesson 2 in Notebook flipchart in Appendix B3.2) and showed a crime scene photograph. Students were asked to come up to the board,

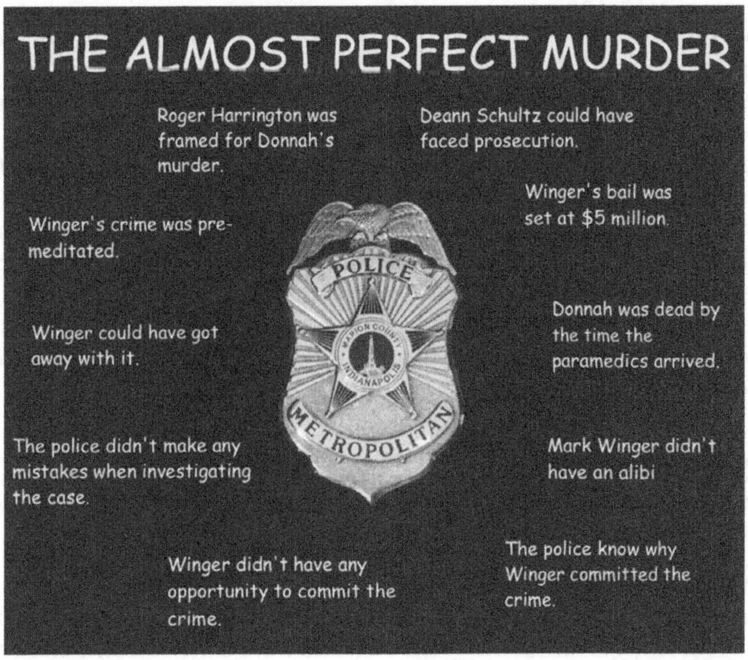

Figure 3.2 'Badge of Truth' activity

circle what they would investigate and explain why, again with verbalization of reasoning being central to the process. See **Video 17** of this activity.

Lesson 3

The final lesson drew together work from previous lessons so that students started to plan their crime stories. The starter activity was a multiple choice Flash tool 'recap' quiz. Students came to the board to select their chosen answer, with feedback being provided immediately by the quiz tool. They were then provided with a selection of three 'prop' items on their tables, which they used to form an idea for a crime story – again promoting group discussion and building upon each other's ideas. Typical crime story structures and adaptations were discussed as a whole class (see Slide 5 in Lesson 3 flipchart in Appendix B3.3) and a sample planning grid was displayed on the IWB. Students then worked on devising their own plans. At the end, they moved to work with a partner of their choice (friendship groupings) to share their initial ideas and support each other with developing them further. (See Appendices B3.1, B3.2 and B3.3 for copies of IWB Notebook pages used for all three lessons.)

Research plan

Teacher participants and researchers worked together in a series of workshops, sharing our experiences and evolving our construction of 'dialogue'. (See Chapter 2 for more details of methods and background literature.) The sequence of three lessons was videoed and the teachers involved in the project kept diaries recording pre- and post-lesson reflections and planning. I and the other participating teachers were interviewed by a member of the research team about our plans and again after lessons. Flipchart files and captured annotations, lesson plans, worksheets, digital photographs and copies of student work provided additional data.

Subsequent analysis of the data was carried out by researchers in collaboration with each teacher participant. In addition, students from my teaching group completed a written questionnaire eliciting their views on the use of the IWB and of dialogue in the classroom.

Research findings

The findings are presented under the three research questions which framed this study.

Findings from a teaching perspective

How can I, as a teacher with a firmly established dialogic approach, exploit the multimodality and interactivity of the IWB to support student learning?

The following features of a supportive environment emerged:

- Varied use of interactive and multimodal features of the IWB supported co-construction of knowledge and understanding in these lessons.
- A supportive environment for risk-taking, where students were given options of discussion group size (pairs/whole table groups) and composition, was created.
- A teaching approach that gave students responsibility for their own learning and fostered willingness to experiment, facilitated dialogue between students, and between students and teachers.
- A mix of exploratory and directive talk on both sides was noted: for example, the teacher being directive in terms of writing genre, and students being directive in terms of evidence collected.
- Examples were noted of dialogue which was 'cumulative' in terms of learners shaping their ideas in relation to others and building collective responses to the evidence base.
- The lessons were seen to offer opportunities for students to develop and articulate their reasoning, directly encouraged by the teacher.

Findings from students' perceptions

What value do students place on the use of the IWB and the use of talk in a classroom setting?

- 74 per cent of students stated that they preferred lessons where the IWB was used, and 26 per cent expressed no preference.
- 87 per cent of students believed that use of the IWB helped them to learn. Some students felt that this was because the IWB was 'more modern and fun'. Others felt the clarity of information was better on the IWB.

- One student commented, 'I think it does help with my learning because the tasks are written on the board, and you can always see what is going on in the lesson.'
- Some students observed that the IWB meant less time was wasted waiting for the teacher to write things up.
- Saving work and returning to it in future lessons was also highlighted as an important advantage.

What insights can students offer in order to help us further support their learning?

- 78 per cent of students felt that talking did help them to learn.
- 57 per cent preferred to choose group composition themselves, 4 per cent wanted the teacher to choose, and 39 per cent liked a mix of the two.
- 60 per cent preferred working in pairs or small groups, 9 per cent liked to work as a whole class, 9 per cent individually and 22 per cent liked a mix.

Discussion, conclusions and recommendations

By focusing on the IWB as a classroom resource to support a dialogic approach, I was able to use this technology in ways that I would not have considered before. The key aspects of IWB use that stand out in this project are, first, its 'motivational' and 'engaging' characteristics, and second, its role in sustaining the continuity of dialogue and learning over sequences of lessons. In terms of supporting teaching and learning, the IWB software means that resources can be prepared in advance, allowing for a faster pace in lessons. Some may argue that this could prevent spontaneity and flexibility, however, the adaptability of the IWB comes into play here: for example, its ability to move forward or back through slides as many times as necessary, amending and adding new slides if required, obviates the need for a 'fixed' lesson plan. The other feature which I have found invaluable and which has also been commented on by students is the fact that work from lessons can be saved and then used again or referred back to in future lessons, and this function can be used both within and across teaching groups.

In terms of dialogic teaching, this small-scale study's findings illustrate how the IWB can be used effectively to support this approach. The student data, in particular, highlights the value of collaborative ways of working that involve articulating ideas and co-constructing knowledge. Students' preferences for group size and composition were interesting but it should be noted that this group was comprised of high-achieving, motivated and relatively independent learners who were already used to using talk as a tool for learning. For effective dialogue to take place, regardless of resources used to promote it, classroom climate and the establishment of ground rules and agreed ways of working are paramount. Just as students need support with how to read and write effectively, they also require support with the structures for effective and meaningful talk.

Evaluation and reflection

This project has further convinced me of the value of dialogic teaching and that the IWB can be a powerful resource to help support this approach. This is by no means saying that this is the only approach and tool to be used, but rather that they can form an important and valuable part of a teacher's 'toolkit'. On reflection, none of the activities devised was technologically complicated, but for me, this is just one of the benefits of the IWB – the simplest of uses can be extremely effective. The key points that emerged from a teaching perspective were that the IWB certainly supported learner engagement and motivation, and aided me in terms of both lesson preparation and flexibility during lessons. Its ability to allow for cumulative working is also a real strength. In a follow-up questionnaire, the majority of students involved in the project stated that they valued both the IWB and dialogue as tools to enhance learning. As this is surely at the heart of all we do as teachers, it is this that I feel makes this approach an important one within my teaching repertoire.

Acknowledgements

Many thanks to Julia Flutter for her careful editing of this chapter and to all the children in my school who participated in the study.

Reference

Mercer, N. (1995) *The Guided Construction of Knowledge: Talk Amongst Teachers and Learners*. Clevedon and Philadelphia, PA: Multilingual Matters.

Appendices

(Electronic versions only, available at http://tinyurl.com/OUPIWB)

Appendix B3.1 Caroline's Lesson 1 IWB Notebook slides
Appendix B3.2 Caroline's Lesson 2 IWB Notebook slides
Appendix B3.3 Caroline's Lesson 3 IWB Notebook slides

4 Using the interactive whiteboard to support dialogic teaching in history: the student perspective

Lloyd Brown

Chapter summary

This chapter reports on a small-scale study examining how the use of interactive whiteboards could enhance student learning in history through dialogic interaction. The study was based on a series of three lessons with Year 9 students on aspects of trench warfare during the First World War.

These lessons were planned following a series of workshops involving teachers and university researchers (further details about the research and workshops are presented in Chapter 2). Of particular interest in my own study were the co-construction of knowledge by teacher and students working together, engaging students through dialogue, the opportunity for two students in the class to act as learning partners, playing a role in evaluating lessons and suggesting ideas for the future. In addition to analysing video recordings of the lessons with the university team, I gathered my own research evidence through two whole-class student questionnaires, two 'learning partner' students watching parts of the lessons with me and commenting, an interview between a university researcher and the two learning partners, and two colleagues in my school commenting on the talk in one part of one of the lessons.

The main findings of the study were:

- Pupils were engaged with the activities devised, and the resulting dialogue was cumulative over time
- The majority of students felt they learned more from discussion than writing in these lessons
- Pupils acting as learning partners offered valuable insights into the teaching and learning in these lessons.

Introduction and focus of the study

While research suggests that dialogue based on dialogic teaching and exploratory talk (described by Knight in Chapter 1) has positive relationships to learning, such dialogue is not common in many classrooms. This study explored the potential of IWB features to encourage the development of dialogic teaching and learning.

Context for the study

The study took place at Chesterton Community College in Cambridge, a co-educational city school of 970 students. The students were a mixed ability Year 9 (ages 13–14 years) class of 30 boys with varied socio-economic backgrounds.

Teaching plan

The lessons focused on what sources can reveal about the experience of trench warfare during the First World War. The key question used to frame the three lessons was, 'How far can we imagine the experience of trench warfare?' This question prompts higher-order thinking as students have to evaluate the usefulness of sources in helping them to respond. The sequence of lessons was designed to be cumulative in nature, building on knowledge as we worked through ideas, within the frame of the key question. Central to the collaborative nature of the work were the annotations made to the prepared flipcharts that we could refer back to across lessons (Appendices B4.1 and B4.2). This emphasizes an important advantage of the IWB: the chance to capture student annotations and use them again, so making it easier to build collaborative thinking beyond one lesson.

The first activity involved students analysing Wilfred Owen's poem, 'Dulce Est Decorum Est', to encourage thinking about the experience of war. Following analysis of a YouTube film of the poem, students were asked to consider how *they* would dramatize the poem. The next lesson built on this work, starting with students using mini-whiteboards to draft and discuss a storyboard for their film (Figure 4.1). These ideas were then shared on the IWB (Figure 4.2). One of the lesson objectives, which I wanted students to try to guess at the end, was, 'to think about the advantages of changing one's mind'. Here, I

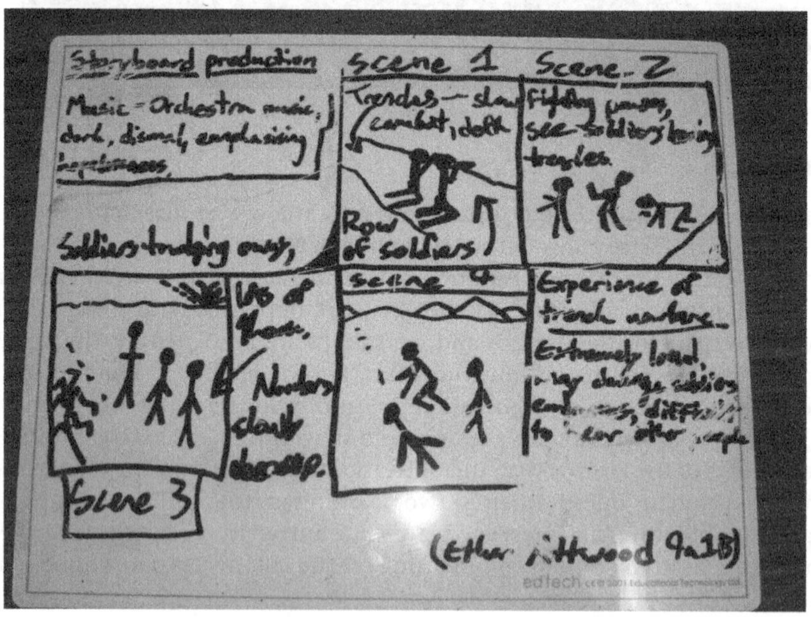

Figure 4.1 Sample storyboard on mini-whiteboard

wanted to ask whether the discussion on storyboards had resulted in anyone changing their minds about the best way to dramatize the poem. After considering both the YouTube clip, and their own thoughts on dramatization, students were asked to reflect on a selection of images that appear when the title of Owen's poem is searched on 'Google images'. The earlier work was intended to boost students' confidence to enable them to comment on whether the images found were appropriate matches for the poem.

Next, I planned to use the 'going over the top' attack scene in the film, *Paths of Glory*. I wanted to play this first with just sound and then secondly with the video images and no sound to help consider

Figure 4.2 Pair shares their storyboard with the class

what we might miss from the audio track of a film. This part of the lesson was framed by the question, 'Is it possible for us to imagine the experience of trench warfare?' This challenged students to consider 'how far' one can put oneself in the position of someone in the past. I felt a dialogic approach to this would generate ideas that all students could use. Furthermore, these ideas would not be found in more traditional texts. At this point I began to record student thoughts on a blank flipchart page to act as a record. The final task involved looking at trench warfare in other ways, including sketching a trench, sketching one collaboratively on the IWB and using original trench images and a diagram. This activity was framed by the question, 'Was there a "typical trench"?'

The last part of the lesson would be an opportunity for students to give their views on what the objectives of the lesson were. I planned to put these hidden on the board beforehand. Did students agree on what the objectives were and did they agree with me on what they were? This seemed an appropriate ending in view of the emphasis on co-construction of knowledge. The ideas built up in this set of activities were used in the third lesson to answer the key question, 'How far can we imagine the experience of trench warfare?' The third lesson was difficult to plan as I was uncertain of the outcomes from Lessons 1 and 2. The use of the IWB allowed me to refer back to use the materials from these two lessons in the third and thus to adjust the plan.

Research plan

Teacher participants and researchers worked together in a series of workshops, sharing our experiences and evolving our construction of 'dialogue'. (See Chapter 2 for more details of methods and background literature.) The sequence of three lessons was videoed and I and the other participating teachers kept diaries recording our pre- and post-lesson reflections and planning. We were also interviewed by a member of the research team about our plans and again after lessons. Flipchart files and captured annotations, lesson plans, worksheets, digital photographs and copies of student work provided additional data.

Subsequent analysis of the data was carried out by researchers in collaboration with each teacher participant. One researcher and myself each selected 'critical episodes' from the video records independently. This helped us to identify what the evidence revealed about the integration of IWB use with teacher–student and student–student dialogue. It also gave us an opportunity to reflect on whether there was any 'added value' from this approach. We were joined for part of the discussion by two learning partner students who were able to expand on the thoughts they had articulated in previous discussion with the teacher. All of this helped us to agree on a final set of 'critical episodes' for the sequence of lessons and some ideas for our understanding of dialogic learning with the IWB. One particular interest for me in this project was the role of the student as learning partner. My interest developed from a previous project in school in 2007, in which students had worked with teachers on planning and evaluating lessons. There was much to learn from this and I have been very interested in an opportunity for further similar work which the current project provided. In addition, students were given two complementary questionnaires to complete, the first after Lesson 2, comprising the following statements for students to give written responses to:

1. I have an opportunity to influence the learning of others.
2. I have opportunities to give my view.
3. Others in the class listen to my point of view.
4. Mr Brown listens to our points of view and uses them.
5. I have learned more from what I have written than from what has been discussed.

Research findings

There are a number of findings from this research although one must be careful about extrapolating too far from such a small-scale study. The findings all lead to the prompting of further questions and the need to test any provisional results.

First, it seems that this group of students believes that they learned more from discussion than from writing in these lessons; responses to the fifth question in the first questionnaire indicated that of the 21 students responding:

- Four thought they learned about the same amount from both the discussion and writing.
- None felt they had learned more from writing.
- Fifteen felt they had learned more from discussion.

Few of the written responses went far beyond this simple judgement, and a follow-up question to understand more about the meaning of this response would have been useful. However, some students said that discussion helps their learning because they can 'get ideas from other people'. One noted that 'from writing I have learnt most of the facts and dates, but through discussion I have learnt other theories and points of view and seen things from a different angle'. This suggests another line of enquiry exploring whether students think facts are best recorded on paper while second-order concepts of history might be best learned through a more open dialogic approach.

These responses support other survey work I have been involved with in school. We asked 101 students from different teaching groups the same question last year and 74 responded that they learned more from discussion. Twenty-six respondents were Key Stage 4 students (aged 14–16) and more of them suggested they learned more from writing. However, the explanation for this had a number of students noting that they knew they would need what they had written later to help them do well in exams.

A second outcome is that the learning partners work has made me reassess my own thinking about a 'dialogic lesson' and particularly the role of the teacher within it. When watching the videoed lessons with the two students, they expressed strong views that too much of the discussion was mediated by the teacher. I feel this is an accurate reflection in some senses. The activities and timings of the lesson were set by the teacher. While I attempted to have minimal say in the findings that students came up with to frame our discussions, I can see that for students, this may have seemed like a traditional teacher-led lesson in some ways, with the teacher setting the tasks and organizing the collation of ideas. They felt a more unstructured approach to dialogue would be more powerful. As a result, we planned a later lesson together on whether democracy was a better method of government than dictatorship. One of the students, in his reflections on this lesson, felt that the more unstructured approach, with more dialogic class discussion, led to students being able to build well on each other's ideas and more effectively than in the three-lesson sequence for the project.

The two students involved in the learning partners project also commented that I could challenge the views of students more. It is true that in the three lessons, I challenge views infrequently, although one student suggested in his survey return that I do 'improve' views that are 'bad'. I was more concerned in the lessons with gathering together the thoughts of as many students as possible, to allow everyone the opportunity to reflect for themselves on these. Robin Alexander's (2008) survey of international research on classroom talk highlights that in continental Europe teachers are 'more honest' in their feedback to children than those in England. He suggests that it is often common for a child's contribution to be praised regardless of its appropriateness or quality, so as not to discourage the child. Perhaps the two students see a need for the teacher to be more judgemental in order for them to progress further.

There is certainly merit in this argument, although contextual information is important when considering the best approach. These were almost my first lessons with this class and so confidence-building for the students was very important to me. However, perhaps some of the students want more synthesis of views from the teacher. The survey returns suggest I do use the views of students. But they do not suggest whether or not students would like to be guided more to a particular answer. My hunch on this would be that most students from the group would not, but it is worth further investigation.

Overwhelmingly, students felt the activities suited their learning style. They were engaged and enjoyed the lessons. They commented on the usefulness of mini-whiteboards, the IWB and discussing things with others. I was somewhat surprised from the surveys at how many students said that they learn from the ideas of others in discussion. This is, for me, a very positive finding from the work, and needs to be shared with other colleagues in school and analysed further.

Discussion, conclusions and recommendations

Having worked on the T-MEDIA project, another collaborative project with other schools, and on this study, I am confident about the benefits of using the IWB as one way to improve classroom dialogue. The student feedback suggests that they engaged well with the activities and enjoyed the lessons. However, one must be careful not to extrapolate too much from such a small-scale and short-term study. Written work produced from the lessons was not particularly different in terms of quality from work produced using more traditional resources. But the opportunities for reflection by the students on the lessons may have helped them to be more active participants in the learning process. This could be beneficial in the future if returned to.

The lesson activities are adaptable, I believe, for many other learning situations in history and other disciplines too. I believe the strategies are useful in any curriculum area where an investigative, problem-solving approach is taken. The different resources and strategies service the learning rather than the other way round and, therefore, in my judgement, could be applied across the curriculum.

There are many questions that could be explored further. As I said earlier, it would be interesting to research further on why many of the students involved think they learn more from discussion than writing. Also, what kinds of learning do they think happen in discussion? Are these more important to them? I think it would be valuable to look at the questions that work best in framing dialogue. Also, what is the role of the teacher in the dialogic learning situation? What is an effective balance between positive reinforcement and challenge that moves on student thinking?

All of these questions come from my reflections on participation in the study. They are important in furthering the development of teaching and learning in our school, which should be something that comes from this study. This is important given that, despite the importance of dialogue in learning (see Chapter 1), there is a paucity of high-quality dialogue in classrooms; working to understand why this is the case, and to encourage colleagues to engage in dialogic approaches may be an important step in developing whole-school teaching and learning.

Evaluation and reflection

Working with a group of committed, intelligent, thought-provoking colleagues who all want to see teaching and learning develop has been a richly rewarding experience. The group itself worked in a very dialogic way and this was important to the success of the workshops. The definition of dialogue that we developed and revised contains many words and phrases that we discussed within the group which motivated me towards what we were trying to do.

My understanding of dialogue has developed. I have been able to clarify some things. For example, I am more certain about the value of co-constructing knowledge and understanding in the classroom. I have thought about new aspects to dialogic learning that I had not particularly considered previously. A willingness to change one's mind in discussion was probably already an implicit part of my understanding of dialogic talk, but the project has emphasized its importance.

Some questions are, of course, unanswered. For example, can we actually move a whole group of students to a common understanding of something and be confident that they have that common understanding? Is this even more difficult when one employs the open-ended approach implicated in the dialogic approach described? Is it even desirable or is it sufficient to stimulate all students to expand their own knowledge and thinking in a new direction, but not necessarily towards an identical outcome? The project has also helped me think about the meaning of 'knowledge'. If a teacher has a belief that children can create historical knowledge through dialogue, what is the status of that knowledge? These are the kinds of issues one should continue to wrestle with in one's professional development. Furthermore, if you take a questioning approach to your own practice, you continue to grow professionally yourself. The project has reminded me that educational research will often lead to more questions than firm conclusions.

There has been significant use of IWB technology at our school. By the end of this year, all classrooms will have IWBs. In some, teachers are using them to support dialogue. In others they can sometimes be used to prevent it. The school has already held a research conference centred on dialogic teaching and there is a commitment among a growing group of colleagues to develop classroom talk. We have made a promising start and this project can now suggest how the IWB can enhance dialogic learning. I hope dissemination of this work can help colleagues ask new questions about the talk in their classrooms.

Acknowledgements

Many thanks to Simon Knight for his careful editing of this chapter, and to all the learners who participated in the study in my school. I am also grateful to my school colleagues who helped me to analyse the talk in my lessons.

Reference

Alexander, R. (2008) *Towards Dialogic Teaching: Rethinking Classroom Talk,* 4th edn. Cambridge: Dialogos.

Appendices

(Electronic versions only, available at http://tinyurl.com/OUPIWB)

B4.1 Lessons 1–2 Flipcharts
B4.2 Lesson 3 Flipchart

5 Supporting dialogue by exploiting interactive features of the IWB

Sara Hennessy

Chapter summary

The interactive whiteboard (IWB) can support student learning through classroom dialogue if teachers exploit its interactive features effectively. The technology opens up opportunities for learners to generate, share, refine and evaluate new ideas, through 'multimodal' interaction with a wide variety of digital media resources (e.g. audio, video, photographs, simulations and animations) at the board, along with talk. Using the IWB can thereby support rich new forms of dialogue that highlight differences between perspectives and make learners' ideas and reasoning processes more explicit.

'Digital artefacts' – objects or texts collaboratively produced and manipulated by teachers and learners – can play a pivotal role here. A collective representation of the knowledge that is developing in the class can be displayed on the IWB. It serves as a visible record of ongoing activity and a rich resource for further teaching and learning. When a class interacts with digital artefacts, learners can scrutinize new ideas and develop them over time to build knowledge.

The account is illustrated with examples from case studies of primary and secondary school practice (many of which are also summarized in the Resource Bank, with supporting flipchart examples in the IWB Template files). Analysing sequences of lessons has illuminated how teachers can exploit the IWB through cumulative interaction with a succession of linked digital resources and through archiving and revisiting earlier artefacts. The IWB thereby helps to support the progression of dialogue over time and across settings.

Introduction: the IWB as a tool to support 'multimodal' interaction

The interactive whiteboard is a popular and unique form of classroom technology. It is perceived as being well suited to support interactive whole class teaching (Thomas and Cutrim-Schmid 2010), in contrast with traditional whole-class teaching, which has tended to use computers and other technologies for demonstration purposes. In this chapter I argue that the particular features of the IWB offer some significant advantages for the dialogic teacher and I show how these features might be most effectively exploited; the value of any tool is of course entirely dependent on how it is used. The IWB makes a very effective presentation tool but unless it is used in a genuinely interactive way, it is merely a very expensive form of 'glorified overhead projector', as one teacher described it.

The IWB technology comprises a large, touch-sensitive electronic board that is visible to an entire class through use of a data projector. It is linked to a desktop or laptop computer but allows direct input and interaction with resources on the computer via finger or stylus. The computer not only drives the projector but also runs the specialized software that comes with each manufacturer's board (e.g. SMART Notebook or ActivInspire) and supports interaction with resources on the board in ways that were not previously possible. The set-up means that objects and texts can be easily created, moved or transformed by teachers or learners.

Unlike most other current forms of educational technology and software, the IWB is a *generic* classroom tool. It provides an unrestricted portal for interaction with an infinitely wide range of secondary digital resources, especially when linked to a computer with Internet access. This offers teachers tremendous ease and flexibility in sourcing materials to stimulate dialogue.

The IWB additionally allows *multimodal* interaction with a wide range of digital media resources. These include texts, photographs, multimedia presentations, animations, simulations and models, interactive diagrams, spreadsheets and databases, graphs and charts, tables, web pages, maps, and audio and video files. Using such visual and dynamic representations helps to make complex subject concepts and processes more explicit, concrete and transparent. These representations can communicate meaning less abstractly than talk alone (Wells 1999: ch. 4) because they are usually publicly interpreted through teachers' and students' speech, gaze and gesture at certain points during the course of activity. This interpretation of resources on the IWB offers a wealth of information about a topic all at once, with opportunities to check understanding and provide clarification. Teachers can thus use the IWB to support reasoning activities including visualizing or modelling a problem or process.

The specialized tools for directly manipulating digital objects provided as part of the IWB software package offer significant 'added value' here, above and beyond other technology uses. They include tools for annotating text or images, highlighting, drawing, hide-and-reveal, re-sizing and zooming. These functions can help to draw attention to salient features of a representation or process.

For example, in one science case study described by Hennessy et al. (2007), the teacher, Chris Tooley, introduced the process of gaseous exchange at the alveoli (the primary gas exchange unit of the lungs) by annotating a diagram (Figure 5.1), animating it, and then describing it to help students develop a vivid mental image of a dynamic process: 'You can see the red blood cells all moving round the capillary . . . What's coming in now [as you're breathing in] is just showing you the oxygen content . . .' (p. 292).

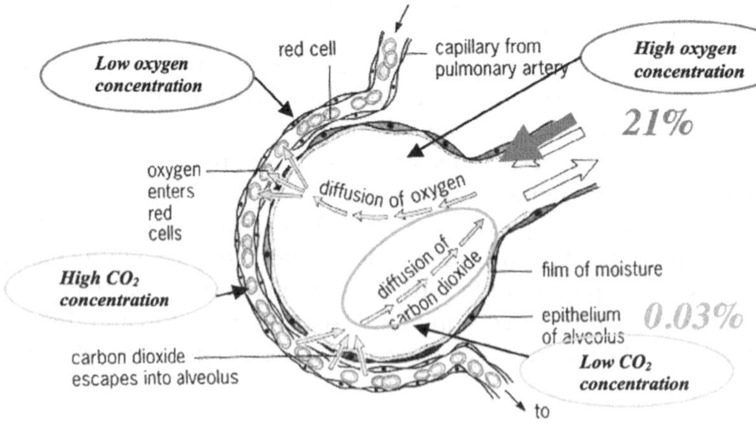

Figure 5.1 Gaseous exchange in the alveoli

Chris used questioning to check understanding and occasionally drew on student responses to provide key information. Use of the annotation tool helped to scaffold and record the developing shared understanding of gaseous exchange. He animated the static diagram to illustrate the simultaneous processes, exploiting the stop–start facility to break the system into manageable steps for learning. His intention was for students to understand complex processes by 'picturing themselves in the situation' and 'seeing it in perspective', using images as 'visual cues' while he discussed them:

> So that picture we just saw, that's me standing here and looking back towards the bronchial tube. Now that's one where the alveoli has been cut open so you can see all those little bubbles. Here's a picture of what it really looks like . . . some sort of seaweed . . . And you can see that running over these alveoli are capillaries carrying blood. (Ibid., p. 292)

Pupils were not simply passive viewers; they were expected to engage in dialogue and reasoning with peers to formulate a theory about how the structural features of the alveoli facilitated gaseous exchange, including: 'Where does the carbon dioxide come from that gets into the lungs when you breathe out?... The oxygen that's taken out of the alveoli . . . what's carrying it away?...How is that whole dynamic process working?' (Ibid., p. 293).

The IWB software tools can also be used in jointly constructing or deconstructing texts and other artefacts to create new ones. For instance, Figure 5.2 depicts an example of a secondary English class transforming a poem. The sequence of slides illustrates how the original text was 'fragmented' or 'disappeared' (Jewitt 2011) in the course of a developing dialogue around it. The dialogue explored: a character's feelings, the significance of an evocative image (second slide) for the poem's persona, and the ways in which the image and poem, plus other poems studied, might reflect today's society. Learners' own interpretations were captured through exploiting the IWB's facilities for direct manipulation, highlighting and annotating images and texts during discussion.

Such IWB activity illustrates the 'added value' of the IWB over a computer and data projector alone. Some parts of this activity and the others described in the chapter could potentially be carried out without the technical interactivity of the IWB. However, exploiting the added functionality and the immediate responsiveness that the tool offers can significantly extend and enrich the experience.

Exploiting the IWB to support whole-class dialogue

Collective knowledge-building

Interactive whiteboard use can support collaborative knowledge-building by a class through constructing texts and objects within its proprietary software environments. This knowledge-building process is again aided by the specialized tools provided. 'IWB use helps to make differences between perspectives more explicit while understanding is developing' (Hennessy 2011). It supports dialogue because different ideas can more easily be juxtaposed, highlighted, explored, connected and contrasted, and their strengths and weaknesses become more salient. It opens up a fluid shared communication space and new opportunities for learners and teachers publicly to express, explain, justify, evaluate and reformulate ideas – both orally and using other representations. Interactive whiteboard use can thereby open up a space for rich, multimodal forms of classroom dialogue that go beyond verbal dialogue.

New dialogues can evolve around what I call 'digital artefacts' (Hennessy 2011) – objects or texts jointly created and manipulated by teachers and learners on the IWB, again in conjunction with talk, gaze and gesture. Digital artefacts make words and ideas themselves available for manipulation – as 'improvable objects' (Wells 1999). These may be iteratively developed through collective scrutiny and collaborative activity by a class. These external, dynamic representations of knowledge within objects constructed and manipulated on the board offer support for the processes of collective knowledge-building, question-posing and inquiry. Such artefacts can be simple constructions such as a text or diagram; research shows that advanced or 'whizzy' uses of the IWB technology are unnecessary for learning and fairly prosaic uses (e.g. displaying a question and recording students' responses around it) can actually be remarkably effective.

Supporting cumulative dialogue

By making both learning histories and trajectories more visible, including tracking them over time, digital artefacts can additionally help dialogue to progress cumulatively and thus to continue during a lesson or between lessons. These collectively produced knowledge objects are provisional; they provide interim

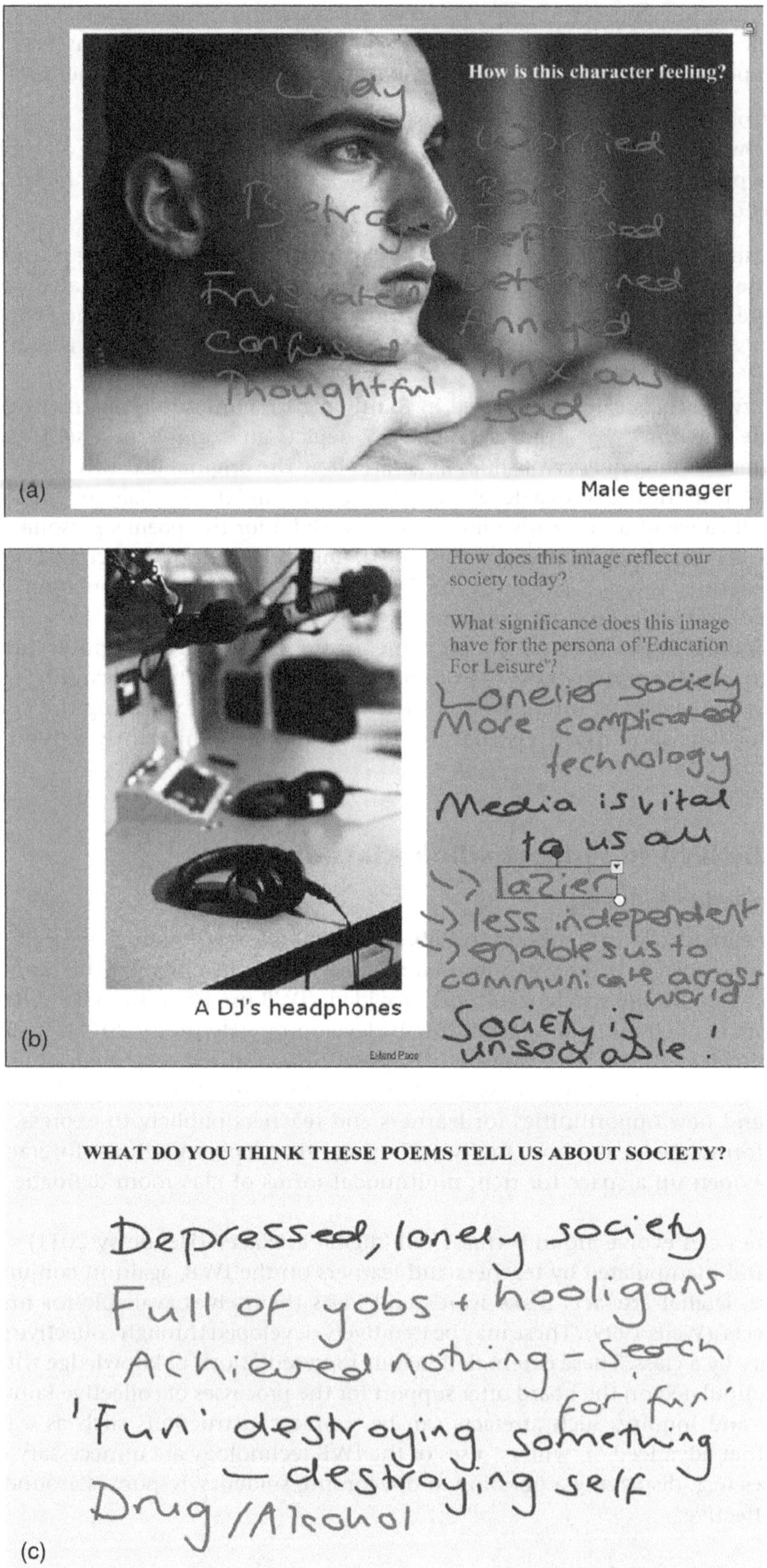

Figure 5.2 Series of IWB slides used during an English lesson on the poem 'Education for Leisure' by Carol Ann Duffy: (a) Describing a teenager's feelings; (b) Linking an image to a poem's persona; (c) Brainstorming the messages about society

records of the creative process, evolving to become rich resources for the group later on. Classroom activities can be intentionally designed to require students to respond to their peers' ideas and thus to support dialogue. For example, when a class progressively builds a food chain, each student adds a link that builds on the previous contribution, communicates their reasoning and contributes to the final outcome. Another example was described in Part A, Section 2.4 (IWB activity 1) where successive students graphically annotated a digital photograph of a historical portrait.

A further example comes from the sequence of three history lessons on trench warfare described in Part A, Section 2.4, IWB activity 3. In the third lesson, a trench diagram (Figure 5.3) was drawn (side-on view) by six students in turn each cumulatively adding elements perceived to be typically present. It contained an imaginative range of such elements and succinctly portrayed rather more than was stated verbally, since the diagram itself conveyed the learners' perspectives. The artefacts they drew, along with the dialogue depicted in IWB activity 3, encapsulated much of the rich multimodal experience and pair/class dialogue of the previous two lessons, with students referring to the DVD and other digital resources they had encountered: in their drawing they were 'building on their informed speculation from some of the things that they had seen' (Lloyd).

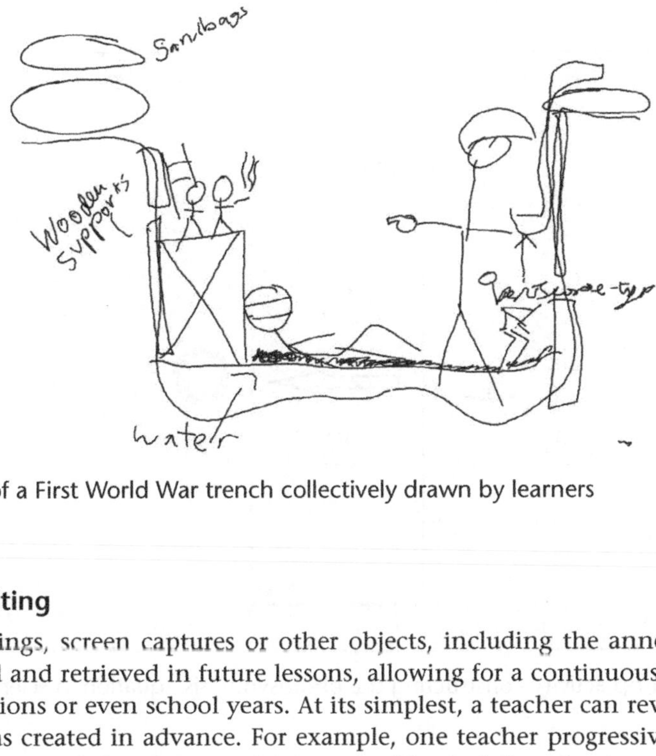

Figure 5.3 Diagram of a First World War trench collectively drawn by learners

Archiving and revisiting

Importantly, all drawings, screen captures or other objects, including the annotated or manipulated versions, can be saved and retrieved in future lessons, allowing for a continuous thread of interactions across many class sessions or even school years. At its simplest, a teacher can revisit with a class digital resources that s/he has created in advance. For example, one teacher progressively built up – over six lessons – a representation of the photosynthesis cycle (Figure 5.4), using images of its components, revisiting earlier elements in each subsequent revision, as detailed by Hennessy et al. (2010)[1]. Accompanied by practical investigation, this pivotal use of the equation helped students to explore and understand the role of each core element in the overall photosynthesis process.

Alternatively, jointly constructed artefacts may be revisited. The first two annotated slides shown in Figure 5.2 were returned to in the subsequent lesson, in order to bridge between lessons. This revisiting pulled together ideas from the two poems studied and refocused students, allowing them constant reference to their earlier ideas and thoughts. These slides reminded learners of what they already knew and provided a springboard for further discussion of the themes depicted.

Both of these examples were *teacher-initiated revisiting* that clearly depended on significant advance preparation in collating previous resources. In our study of IWB use in Caroline Neale's middle school English classroom, many *students* asked for slides depicting typical crime story structures and adaptations from an earlier lesson to be displayed again in order to support development of their own crime stories. In the history lesson sequence on trench warfare outlined above, students also requested access to earlier resources: 'When we were writing our piece on World War I we had everything on the IWB and we were constantly going up and flicking through it' (Danny).

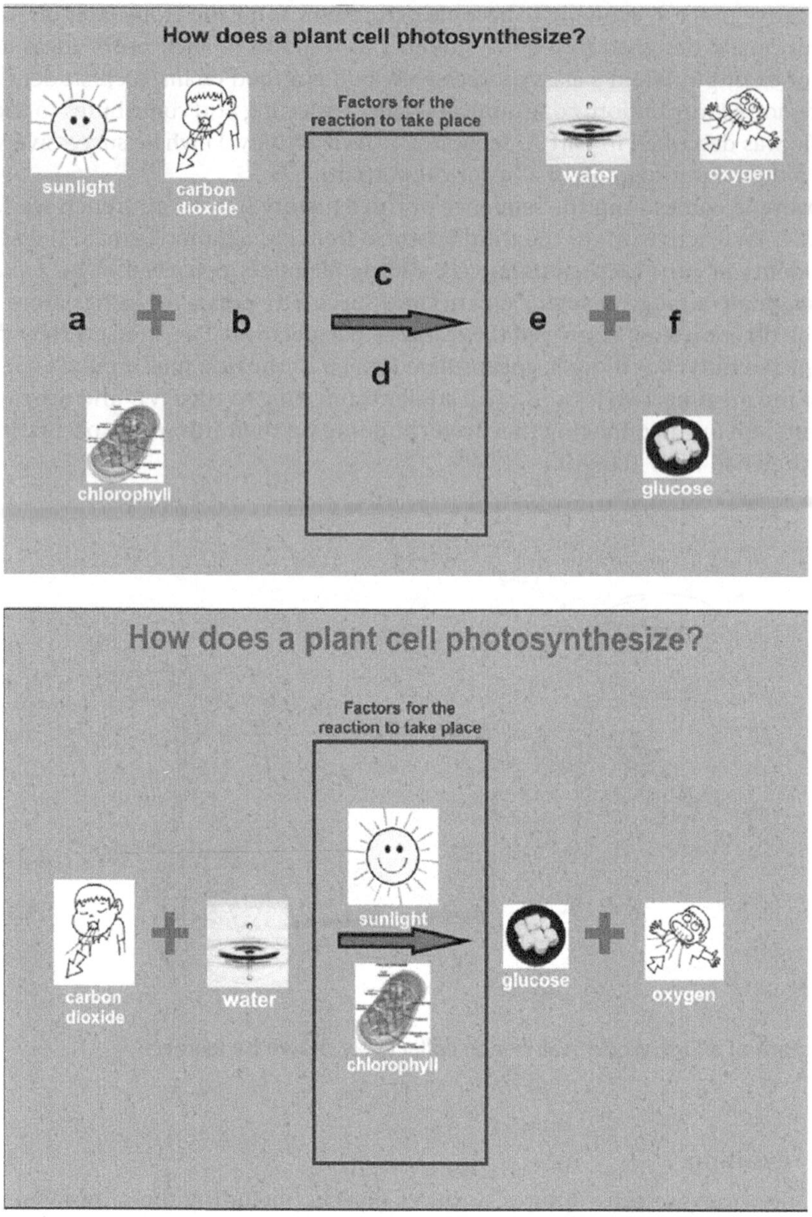

Figure 5.4 Drag-and-drop activity constructing the photosynthesis equation in science

Despite their shared ownership, IWB artefacts are usually less accessible after the lesson to students than to teachers (who are the gatekeepers), however. The use of the IWB as a potential repository of resources for student access is uncommon, possibly for practical reasons, but might be explored.

'Revisiting' may also be extended to include interacting with digital artefacts created by experts in the topic area or by other groups of learners, for various purposes – perhaps as scaffolding, as a stimulus to provoke thinking and make explicit learners' own views in response, or again to explore difference between perspectives across groups as well as within. For example, during our pilot filming in Lloyd Brown's classroom, we observed him display a spider diagram depicting a brainstorm from another class about 'how wars start' (Figure 5.5) for comparison and contrast with the class's own ideas.

Finally, in concept or mind mapping, students might use key terms from a set and drag and drop them, draw arrows, and/or add text to make connections and explain key ideas about a topic (Figure 5.6). Results can be saved and added to throughout a lesson or across lessons on a particular topic. Learners could make a mind map at their desks before or during the class activity. They could also do the activity at the beginning and end of a lesson or lesson sequence to illustrate what they have learned. Model mapping is especially useful for children with literacy difficulties.

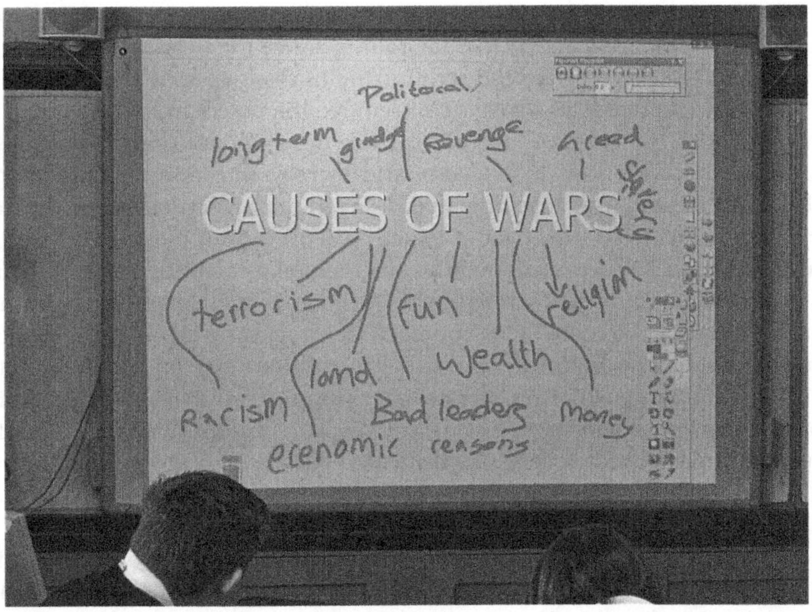

Figure 5.5 Revisiting a brainstorm

Creating concrete representations of ideas on the IWB and receiving feedback allows learners to reflect productively on their own explanations and others' critical perspectives on those. In sum, the use of IWBs to develop and support student engagement with external 'knowledge objects' can serve to highlight differences between perspectives, to deepen classroom dialogue and to sustain it over time. The onus is on the teacher, however, to draw out children's ideas and explanations.

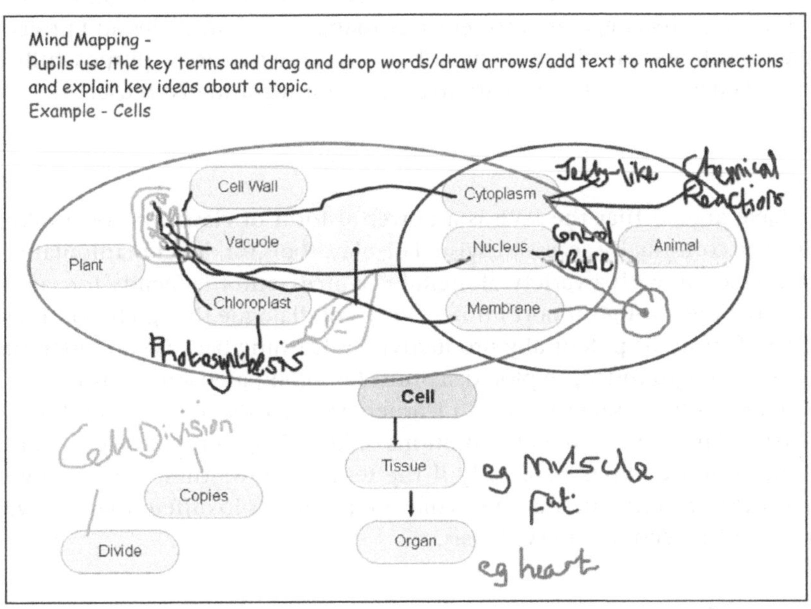

Figure 5.6 An annotated model map of cell features

Extending IWB use

The IWB can be effectively combined with other peripherals such as a document camera – also known as a 'visualizer' or 'digitizer' – where objects placed beneath the camera stand (which can also have a flexible stem) appear on the screen, or even a standard digital camera. Such peripheral cameras can be used to display, critique or compare students' work or experimental results, or to project an image as a task stimulus. Uses devised by primary teachers include rolling a dice for a class to see, showing calibrations on equipment, such as a ruler or syringe, and scrutinizing in close-up view the structure of bread going mouldy. The teacher can also freeze an image, then remove the object from the visualizer and manipulate it, and compare it with the original. In the sequence of secondary science lessons we observed on photosynthesis, the teacher used a flexible document camera to illustrate the branching veins in a leaf and to discuss their role. He also used it during an investigation of whether carbon dioxide is needed for photosynthesis; students predicted the effect of (three days of) carbon dioxide deprivation on a photosynthesizing leaf and the teacher demonstrated the outcome of a starch test using the camera.

The advent of remote input devices (tablets, wireless mice) reduces exposure of learners and releases the teacher from the front of the room. This approach of integrating technologies, where students use handheld computers or remote pointers to interact with IWB content, can add new strategies to engage everyone in IWB-based learning activities. In the example depicted in Figure 5.4, students composed the photosynthesis equation at their desks using colour printed mini-diagrams ('matched resources'), justifying their own arrangements to peers; this generated quite a lot of discussion and reportedly motivated students to 'want to know the answer'. The teacher circulated, talking to small groups of students, questioning and challenging their thinking. One student then came up to the IWB and moved the elements around to complete the equation. Pupils verified their own diagrams against this model before sticking the correct version in their books. **Video 14** shows this activity. Further ideas for engaging all learners in IWB activity are offered in Resource Appendix A7.

The IWB can also act as a focal point for class discussion of displayed observation data in science or mathematics, helping students in a variety of different learning processes: noticing and resolving divergence; considering additional avenues for reflection or observation; grouping ideas together to generate insights about a new topic; reflecting on data or hypotheses; brainstorming limitations to current approaches; or proposing new enquiries (Fong et al. 2012). Discussions carefully facilitated by the teacher are essential to support learning in these contexts.

Finally, new IWB features, technologies and forms of interaction are emerging. For example horizontal multi-touch smart boards and other technologies are now more affordable and available to support collaborative learning within and between groups (Higgins et al. 2011). Group members are able to work simultaneously on such a table device and the focus of attention can again be shifted away from the front of the classroom. Teachers can also centrally manage student tables and project them onto the vertical IWB. As always, however, educators must harness these new tools purposefully as they can also be used mundanely. Pedagogy must be the driving force in integrating IWB use.

Conclusion

In this chapter I have argued that the IWB is a powerful form of classroom technology. Its particular features, including the continually accessible visual display, tools for direct manipulation and highlighting, multimodal interaction with a variety of digital resources, and the facility for saving and revisiting flipcharts, potentially offer strong support for new forms of dialogue that go beyond just talk. Teachers' exploitation of these features is potentially productive for learning because (a) different ideas can more easily be juxtaposed, foregrounded, explored, connected, compared and contrasted, thus rendering strengths and weaknesses more salient, and (b) learners can jointly construct and interact with digital artefacts on the board. These external representations of knowledge provide access to learners' interpretations and current understandings, especially if the teacher draws these out through accompanying oral interaction. At the same time these artefacts may help learners to differentiate between perspectives, supporting further joint reflection and synthesis.

Acknowledgements

Thanks are due above all to the dedicated teachers who willingly participated in the various case studies upon which this chapter is based. The three underpinning research projects[2] were carried out in schools in the East Anglia region of the UK and funded by the UK Economic and Social Research Council. Some of the material in this chapter derives from an article by Hennessy (2011: The role of digital artefacts on the interactive whiteboard in mediating dialogic teaching and learning, *Journal of Computer Assisted Learning*, 27(6): 463–586. doi: 10.1111/j.1365-2729.2011.00416.x) and is drawn upon here by kind permission of the publisher, Wiley-Blackwell.

Notes

1. Video illustrations of how the equation was built up over time and how the teacher managed and structured the activities surrounding it can be seen on the T-MEDIA multimedia science resource at http://t-media.educ.cam.ac.uk (see Clips 1.3, 2.3. 4.2, 5.1).
2. The projects included SET-IT ('Situated Expertise in Technology-Integrated Teaching': R000239823) in 2002–05; T-MEDIA ('Teacher Mediation of Subject Learning with Technology: A Multimedia Approach': RES000230825) in 2005–07; and the 'IWBs and Dialogic Teaching' project (2007–10) on which this resource is mainly based. Reports and publications from each are available at http://www.educ.cam.ac.uk/research/projects/istl/.

References

Fong, C., Pascual-Leone, R. and Slotta, J. (2012) The role of discussion in orchestrating inquiry, paper presented at the International Conference of the Learning Sciences, Sydney. Available at: http://www.isls.org/icls2012/ [accessed 22 May 2012].

Hennessy, S. (2011) The role of digital artefacts on the interactive whiteboard in mediating dialogic teaching and learning, *Journal of Computer Assisted Learning,* 27(6): 463–586. doi:10.1111/j.1365-2729.2011.00416.x.

Hennessy, S., Deaney, R. and Tooley, C. (2010) Using the interactive whiteboard to stimulate active learning in school science, in M. Thomas and E. Cutrim-Schmid (eds) *Interactive Whiteboards: Theory, Research and Practice*. Hershey, PA: IGI-Global.

Hennessy, S., Deaney, R., Ruthven, K. and Winterbottom, M. (2007) Pedagogical strategies for using the interactive whiteboard to foster learner participation in school science, *Learning, Media and Technology,* Special issue on Interactive Whiteboards, 32(3): 283–301. doi: 10.1080/17439880701511131.

Higgins, S.E., Mercier, M., Burd, E. and Hatch, A. (2011) Multi-touch tables and the relationship with collaborative classroom pedagogies: a synthetic review, *Computer-Supported Collaborative Learning,* 6, 515–38. doi:10.1007/s11412-011-9131-y.

Jewitt, C. (2011) The changing pedagogic landscape of subject English in UK classrooms, in K.L. O'Halloran (ed.) *Multimodal Representation and Knowledge*. Routledge Studies in Multimodality Series. New York: Routledge.

Thomas, S. and Cutrim-Schmid, E. (2010) *Interactive Whiteboards: Theory, Research and Practice*. Hershey, PA: IGI-Global.

Wells, G. (1999) *Dialogic Inquiry, Toward a Sociocultural Practice and Theory of Education*. Cambridge: Cambridge University Press.

6 Effective group work at the interactive whiteboard

Paul Warwick

Chapter summary

This chapter will consider classroom conditions for effective learning, making strong links to the dialogic frameworks of understanding outlined in Chapter 1. The teacher will be pictured as being at the heart of mediating not only classroom activities, but also the ethos in which those activities take place.

In considering the place of the IWB in this context, the idea of it as a classroom tool – rather than just a teacher tool – will be presented. In this context group activity at the IWB will be discussed. It will be suggested that the IWB has certain features and perceived benefits of those that make it a suitable tool for use in group activities, and that certain task types lend themselves to such work. However, it will be made clear that if a teacher intends such work to support learning through dialogue, it must be framed within classroom participation structures that not only promote student interaction, but which encourage and develop the use of 'exploratory talk' for learning.

Classroom conditions for effective group work

In Chapter 1 it was made clear by Knight that children do not automatically engage in dialogue in a manner that promotes their learning. We want children to be comfortable working both with the teacher and in groups, reasoning, justifying ideas, acknowledging and repeating the ideas of others, asking focused questions, working towards agreement and elaborating on ideas (Mercer 1996; Barron 2003; Dawes 2004). Yet these are not natural ways of behaving in everyday encounters. Thus the techniques, conventions and attitudes that distinguish effective talk for learning have, themselves, to be learned.

The classroom conditions that support such learning rest very largely on teachers' willingness to promote a classroom ethos and participation structures that supports students making active contributions to lessons. Participation structures can be seen as 'the rights and obligations of participants with respect to who can say what, when and to whom' (Cazden 1986: 437). The point here is that we may intend that children should make an active contribution to class and group interaction, and we may have a classroom ethos that is accepting of children expressing their understandings, but unless we give them the tools to do so, their interactions are likely to be less productive than they might otherwise have been. Thus we must address students' general lack of awareness of the crucial importance of talk for learning. They need to know that there are different kinds of talk and they need a clear understanding that talk for learning involves engaging one another in the sort of discussion that will help everyone to do better than each could alone.

The other component of this view is that students need to be given something interesting to talk about. Tasks need to be conceptually engaging and, if the intention is to promote the kind of dialogue that reveals understanding, tasks should be structured in such a way that students are required to interact and to talk productively. It is here that the IWB has much to offer. As a classroom tool it has been widely used by teachers to extend their 'pedagogic repertoires', the diverse strategies that all teachers have in their armoury and employ as appropriate. This enables not only established ways of teaching to be reinvigorated, but also opens possibilities for new ways of teaching established curriculum content. However, many teachers are looking at the potential of the IWB as more than a 'teacher resource box' (Warwick and Kershner 2008). And while it seems that it is only really in early years classrooms where the consistent use of IWBs by children in individual and group activity has been fully exploited, there is potential for wider use of the IWB for such activity across other phases of schooling.

So what is it about the IWB that seems to lend itself to semi-autonomous group work, and where are there examples of such work?

The IWB as a student tool for learning: examples from science lessons in Key Stage 2 (ages 7–11)

The idea of 'affordances' and 'constraints' has been widely used, with reference to all kinds of educational technology (Kennewell 2001), to express the inherent potential for learning which a digital tool offers. Importantly, for such potential to be realized, it has to be identified by the user. To give an example that is not technology related: to one person a pencil may have affordance for drawing, expressing ideas with variable use of line, shading and pattern; yet another person may perceive it entirely as a tool for writing. The 'flip-side' of affordances is the idea of constraints – in our example, writing with a pencil is not possible without fine motor control. If we apply this to the use of the IWB, there is a very clear relationship between a teacher's pedagogic intentions and the use of the tool. This resource illustrates throughout that a teacher's use of the IWB is intimately bound up with their understanding of teaching and learning – if they have a dialogic intention, they will use the tool in a manner that is likely to promote dialogue. They may, to use one of our examples, see a dialogic affordance in a simple screen shot of Queen Elizabeth I that another teacher may see as an opportunity for a mini-lecture.

In designing 'texts' for interactions in whole-class settings using the generic software of the IWB, teachers have to consider the use of both 'the IWB's capacity to harness a wide... range of multimodal resources in order to facilitate student learning' and 'its capacity to enhance interactive whole class teaching' (Jewitt et al. 2007: 306). Teachers have a critical role when devising an IWB environment that is going to be the basis of a lesson for a particular class of students, in ensuring that it can genuinely enhance the learning experience for them. When preparing a similar resource for use by groups of children there is perhaps an even greater need to consider the learning intentions of the task and how the IWB might help to promote them. It is not that the teacher is likely to be out of the room, or unable to intervene as they might do in any other group work, but it is the case that the stages and purpose of the task should be as clear as possible to the group working at the IWB. In some ways this might be seen as the teacher embedding a 'vicarious consciousness' (Bruner 1986) within the IWB that can guide and support the learners in their activity, when the teacher is not physically present to do so.

The various examples in this resource illustrate clearly that an intimate knowledge of every function of the IWB – or even most of them – is not necessary for it to be used for a dialogic purpose; the Resource Bank begins with some very simple uses. Indeed, sometimes command of the functionality of the IWB can lead simply to an 'all-singing, all-dancing' presentation by the teacher with little regard to the intellectual engagement of their students. But if we think in broad terms about the functionality of the IWB and the generic software that comes with it,[1] it is possible to identify certain features that may assist, or better afford, the intention of dialogic group interaction at the screen.[2]

The 'external memory' of the IWB: the use of the page sorter and page hyperlinks to assist learning

Our first video exemplar of group work at the IWB illustrates how a group of Year 5 children (aged 9–10) engaged in dialogue about where to place a glow-worm in categorizing objects as light sources or reflectors (see **Video 6**).

The excerpt (entitled 'Group interaction at the IWB – light sources and reflectors') – along with the accompanying transcript that can also be found in Appendix B6.1 – provides an example of a group working at a screen where the page sorter was kept open. Another example of such a group activity resource is given in Figure 6.1.

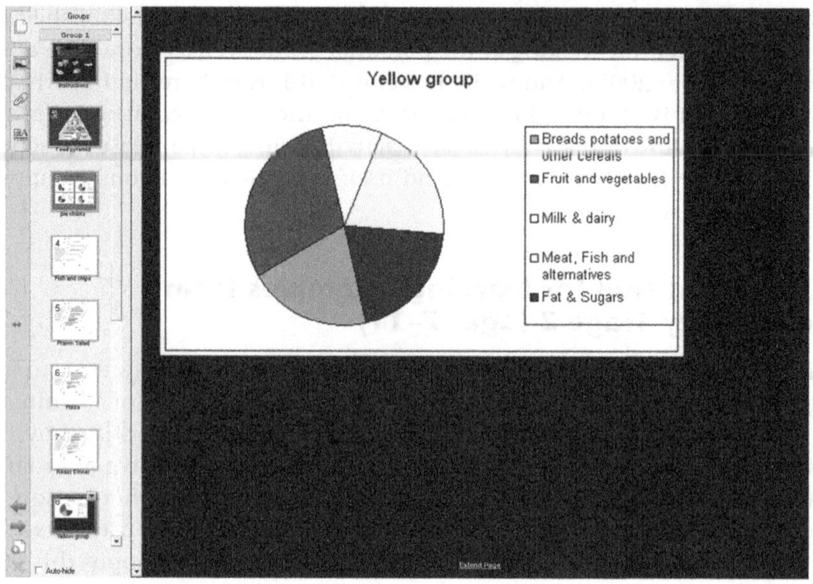

Figure 6.1 Screenshot with the page sorter at the left-hand side

These small versions of the pages that comprise the activities for the lesson might be thought of as acting as an external assistive memory to the learning of the students in both classes – allowing them to, as one student put it, 'flick back pages in your mind'. The lesson that was the basis of Figure 6.1 entailed linking menus with pie charts of food groups. This illustrates an approach in which the students were required to cross-reference different hyperlinked screens to establish the relationships between the menu items and the representation of food groups on the pie charts.

In another class the open page sorter was used rather differently to enable the teacher to sequentially present the task to the students. Again, though differently than in the previously described lesson, the students are provided with an external memory affordance, allowing them to easily return to previous pages in a sequence of interconnected activities. Thus, during the pilot lesson on light and reflectors that features in **Video 6** 'Group interaction at the IWB – light sources and reflectors', the students returned to a previously completed task to change their original responses on the basis of further thinking: 'Can we change something? (*pointing back to previous page*) You know we chose the colour, I don't think it should be blue, I think it should be yellow.'

The students had become aware of the interconnectedness of the activities and the external memory of the open page sorter led to a retrospective revision of the group's initial response. Linked to this, the ability to 'look forward' in the page sorter also seemed to assist this group, allowing them to make connections and move back and forwards through the narrative of the lesson.

In the lesson that features our second video excerpt 'Group interaction at the IWB – food chains' (see **Video 7**) and Appendix B6.2 for the transcript of the excerpt), the page sorter was hidden during each of the lessons. Instead, specific objects and pages were hyperlinked for easy cross-referencing, providing a different form of external memory for the group. In this lesson the central task was to create and justify woodland and pond food chains (see Figure 6.2). Each organism on the page was linked to a 'fact file' that provided some information upon which decisions about positioning within a food chain might be based. The 'vicarious presence' of the teacher was very clearly

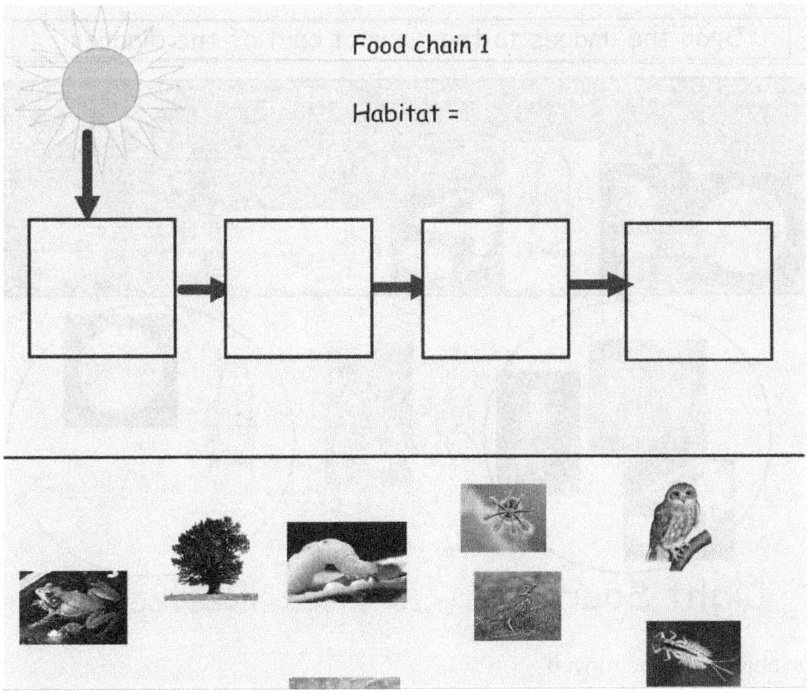

Figure 6.2 Screen shot of food chain activity

embedded in the affordance for learning offered by this hyperlinking but, as in all group work, do not be surprised when the students subvert what you have provided! In this case the students accessed all of the information on the plants and animals systematically, reading them before any attempt was made to place the objects in position on a food chain. Thus, the teacher may have viewed this affordance of the board as working in one way, but the children – working semi-autonomously at the IWB – viewed it differently. This is not a problem of course, unless the anticipated talk is stifled in some way.

Locking and freeing board objects

The degree of freedom for student action in a group task at the IWB is partly determined by the ways in which the teacher chooses to lock down or free objects to be moved. In the food chains video excerpt, for example, it will be clear that the boxes for the food chain were locked in place, while the animal and plant pictures could be moved (it is also clear here, in the case of the line that divides the food chain and the organisms, what can happen when something is not locked when it is supposed to be). In the lesson from which the light sources and reflectors excerpt is extracted, one page appeared as in Figure 6.3 (overleaf).

The students decided to put the picture of the glow-worm in the middle of the two possible groupings to represent their idea that it may be both a light source and a reflector, thus bypassing the template that the teacher had created. This was further elaborated by the students who wrote 'both' underneath the picture, indicated that they have created a new category in addition to the two that the teacher had given them. The teacher had not intended this outcome, as he stated in his written reflection on the lesson: 'This was not a response that I expected to see, but it did lead to more discussion surrounding their placement of the glow-worm on the board.'

Central to the quality of the exchanges in these two lessons is not only the training that the children received in developing exploratory talk, which I will return to, but also the ways in which the teachers had used the twin IWB affordances of provisionality and stability (see also Chapter 5 by Hennessy), evident in the students' handling of screen objects. Stability suggests that, in devising the task, the teacher has determined that some objects (images, words, lines, etc.) are available and in a set position unless the students choose, usually together, to move them. When they are moved, their new position is provisional while *reasons* for the position are discussed, and they are stable in their new position until the group decides to move them again. The IWB thus provides a systematic way of holding and accessing information during the period of collaboration and dialogue.

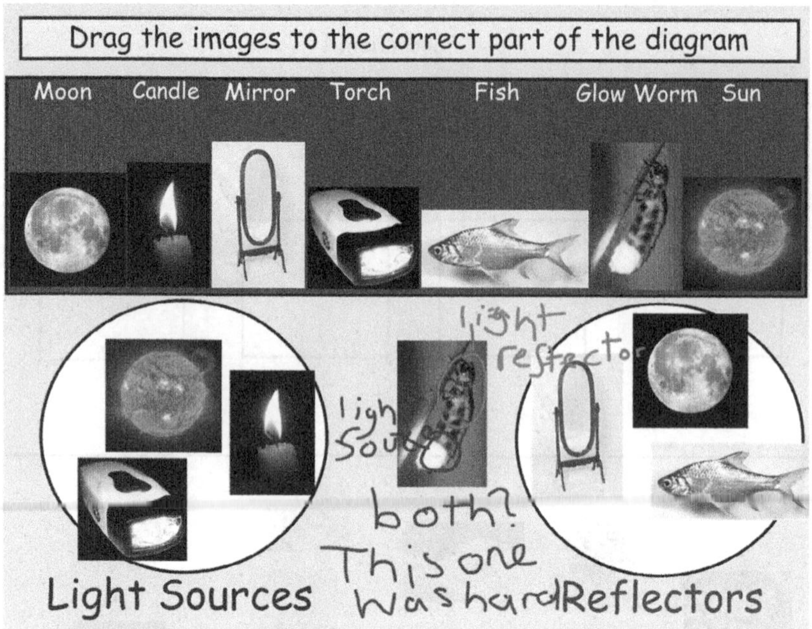

Figure 6.3 Some objects can be moved

Prompts for action

The inclusion of specific instructions, problems, questions or suggestions, or a combination of all four, into IWB task structures, is another generic way in which teachers can vicariously guide a group task. This can be done in several ways:

- the provision of an on-screen question (for example, 'How could you separate a mixture of buttons and sand, a mixture of water and sugar, aluminium cans and iron paper clips?')
- the stating of direct instructions on-screen
- the inclusion of a scenario in which a problem is outlined for the students, usually at the start of each set of pages (one example from our research was where the students were presented with different investigation scenarios and graphs for a dissolving task carried out by another class, but were told that the students in the class had not put their names on the jumbled elements of their work).

One teacher involved in our research employed a rather unique 'Mr H. says' device (Figure 6.4, overleaf), in which his picture appeared on screens with suggestions about what needs to be considered in a particular task. This device was used for direct instruction, to make suggestions about what the task might incorporate, or to give reminders that were linked to earlier spoken instructions.

Such devices enable students to read the prompt collectively and to decide upon how to act upon it. For example, in a prompt that asked students to consider key words for the task, the students ticked off key words used in their task response, articulating what they had done:

S1: 'Opaque' and 'blocks'.

S2: And oh.

S3: And we've done 'light', and we've done 'light'.

S1: Where is, oh yeah 'light's' there. Now we need to say something with a 'straight line'.

Finally in this section on the usefulness of generic IWB affordances for promoting dialogic interaction, it is worth noting that there may be task types that are particularly suited to creating positive learning experiences for student groups. These include: open-ended tasks (e.g. sharing initial topic ideas); a series of cumulative tasks, the pace of which can be controlled by the children (e.g. reviewing previous learning); investigations (in science, history, geography, etc.) and tasks integrating web-based materials (e.g. using web-based simulations and video resources).

Figure 6.4 Screenshot showing the 'Mr. H. says . . .' device

Linking dialogue and learning by groups working at the IWB

The point of the examples above is to illustrate that there are ways of using generic IWB software in the creation of group tasks that are likely to promote dialogue; teachers will be able to think of myriad ways in which this might be done in relation to specific curriculum learning. But it is sensible to return here to the idea that simply providing a task does not necessarily mean that effective talk for learning will happen around it. You will hopefully have noted that, in the examples provided in the two video clips mentioned, the students showed many characteristics of exploratory talk in their interactions; this is not by chance.

Figure 6.5 presents a schematic that expresses the relationship between the key components that might lead to the realization of genuine dialogue by groups at the IWB.

This schematic reflects the idea that the teacher provides a platform of direct and vicarious involvement – in the creation of the task and in the focus on classroom talk rules and procedures (see Chapters 1 and 2) – that enables the opening up of a 'dialogic space' (Wegerif 2007) at the IWB. By creating a participatory classroom ethos, by having a consistent focus on the importance of exploratory talk and by considering how tasks might be structured to create space for talk in the context of the affordances of the IWB, teachers can maximize the use of the IWB as a tool for dialogic learning. In the classrooms where I have worked with teachers, what has been clear is just how important a sustained classroom focus on exploratory group talk is in achieving positive learning outcomes for groups working at the IWB.

With respect to general issues about grouping in classrooms, Baines et al. (2009) provide a wealth of advice that is equally useful when considering the idea of encouraging groups to work at the IWB. But what seems clear in all such work is that where there was little or no sustained emphasis in a classroom on how to talk productively in groups there is likely to be less productive interaction between students, with a consequent effect on learning.

Conclusion

The IWB is an under-used resource if its use is entirely the preserve of the teacher (even with occasional student use as they come up to press something on the board!). Considering its use in the context of group work is not without challenges, but it can provide a highly productive environment for dialogic activity and interaction. In devising such environments a teacher needs to be guided first and foremost by the learning intentions of the lesson and by their own intention to promote dialogic interaction among their students. There are clear affordances of the hardware and software that can be called upon

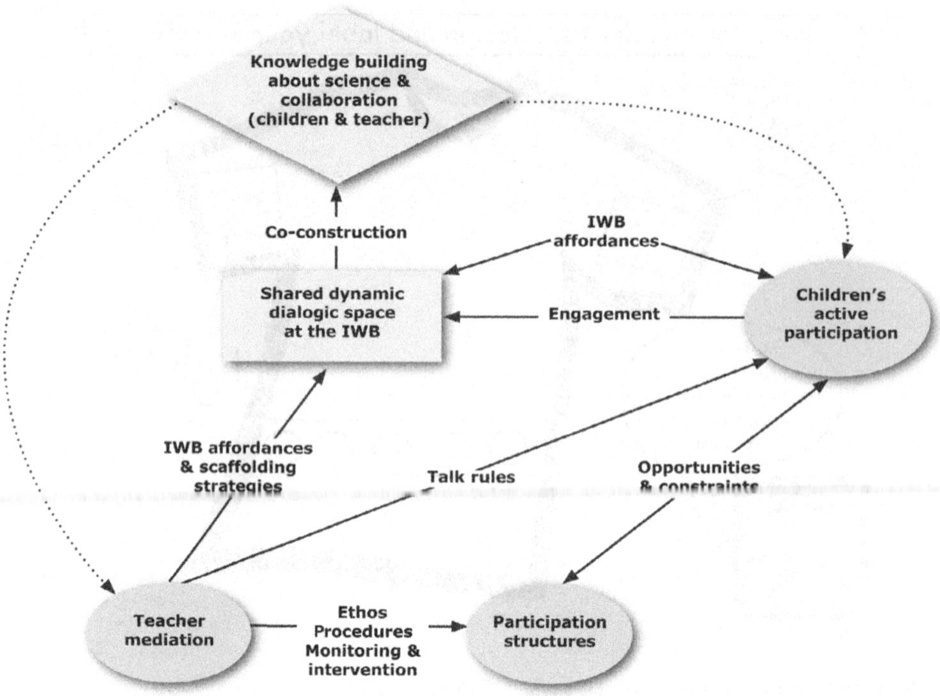

Figure 6.5 Conditions for productive group activity at the IWB (from Warwick et al. 2010)

in devising appropriate tasks for these intentions. However, without a clear and consistent focus on exploratory talk within student groups, the dialogic intentions of any activity at the IWB are likely to be difficult to achieve.

Acknowledgements

The IWBs and Collaborative Pupil Learning in Primary Science project (RES-000-22-2556) was funded by ESRC between 2007 and 2009 and carried out at Faculty of Education, University of Cambridge. More information is available at http://iwbcollaboration.educ.cam.ac.uk/. Thanks are expressed to co-researchers Neil Mercer, Ruth Kershner and Judith Kleine Staarman, and the staff and children of the Cambridgeshire primary schools who gave so freely of their time to the project. The Cambridgeshire ICT service provided a range of help, advice and support.

Notes

1. Notebook, ActivInspire, ActivPrimary, StarBoard software, etc.
2. For more detail on the themes of this chapter, see Warwick et al. (2010); the examples in this section are taken from there.

References

Baines, E., Blatchford, P. and Kutnick, P. (2009) *Promoting Effective Group Work in the Primary Classroom: A Handbook for Teachers and Practitioners*. Abingdon: Routledge.

Barron, B. (2003) When smart groups fail, *The Journal of Learning Science*, 12: 307–59.

Bruner, J. (1986) *Actual Minds, Possible Worlds*. Cumberland, MD: Harvard University Press.

Cazden, C.B. (1986) Classroom discourse, in M.J. Wittrock (ed.) *Handbook of Research on Teaching*, 3rd edn. New York: Macmillan/AERA.

Dawes, L. (2004) Talk and learning in classroom science, *International Journal of Science Education*, 26(6): 677–95.

Jewitt, C., Moss, G. and Cardini, A. (2007) Pace, interactivity and multimodality in teacher design of texts for interactive white boards in the secondary school classroom, *Learning Media and Technology*, 32(3): 303–17.

Kennewell, S. (2001) Using affordances and constraints to evaluate the use of information and communications technology in teaching and learning, *Journal of Information Technology for Teacher Education*, 10(1–2), 101–16.

Mercer, N. (1996) The quality of talk in children's collaborative activity in the classroom, *Learning and Instruction*, 6(4), 359–77.

Warwick, P. and Kershner, R. (2008) Primary teachers' understanding of the interactive whiteboard as a tool for children's collaborative learning and knowledge-building, *Learning, Media and Technology*, 33(4), 269–87.

Warwick, P., Mercer, N., Kershner, R. and Staarman, J.K. (2010) In the mind and in the technology: the vicarious presence of the teacher in pupils' learning of science in collaborative group activity at the interactive whiteboard, *Computers & Education*, 55(1), 350–62.

Wegerif, R. (2007) *Dialogic Education and Technology: Expanding the Space of Learning*. New York: Springer.

7 Learning to learn together with ICT and with the Internet

Rupert Wegerif

Chapter summary

This chapter argues that the key learning skill for the Internet Age is learning how to learn together with others (L2L2). Learning how to learn together is about how students work together and learn from each other with technology like the Internet that supports learning together with others even when the group are not altogether in the same place. The essential attitudes and expectations of L2L2 can be modelled by teachers and taught in much the same way as the Thinking Together approach described in this Reader, Chapter 1, and the dialogic teaching with the IWB that is outlined in Chapter 2 of the main resource (Part A). Some additional strategies apply to supporting learning to learn in groups which raise awareness of the process itself. An illustration of learning to learn together with others via the Internet is offered here along with some tips on how to make this work in practice in your classroom.

Introduction

People have argued that learning to learn is the key skill of the knowledge age as everyone now needs to be flexible and learn new skills throughout their lives. But I think that learning how to learn *together* is also a key skill of the knowledge age since much new learning is done in teams and even when people think that they are learning alone they are often working with others via the Internet. Learning to learn together is not just learning together in a group but also becoming aware of all the things that make learning together with others in groups work. That way the group can learn new things better and also each member of the group can become a better group learner and so go on to be able to learn well in other groups and teams.

Some key aspects of L2L2

Distributed leadership: everyone should feel able to take responsibility for the group's progress and to intervene in order to take the group forward as required. Learning to learn together can involve a move from a clear individual leader to a more distributed leadership pattern. This can be observed through counting the number of idea initiations and looking at their distribution through the group.

Mutual engagement: the members of the group need to listen to each other and share what they know, explaining and checking that their explanations have been understood. Each member of the group should feel able to ask for help and be willing to give help. One subordinate aspect of mutual engagement is to manage conflict.

Peer assessment: groups can effectively judge the quality of their products and members of the group can effectively judge the quality of each other's work; they give constructive formative feedback to each other and to the group as a whole.

Group reflection: groups and group members are aware of the process by which they are deciding on their goals and achieving their goals. They can talk about these processes, processes such as planning out the stages and activities of an inquiry, assuming roles and attitudes towards the work and towards each other and communicating effectively (Wegerif 2013).

Teaching L2L2 requires a change in the role of the teacher, and in the culture of the class or group, that is bigger than any individual lesson plan or educational activity.

Explicit L2L2 objectives and supportive lesson structure

One way to be explicit about L2L2 objectives is to raise them in the introduction to each lesson.

One good lesson structure might be a three-part structure with an introduction reminding the class of their shared expectations for working together and the L2L2 goal for the lesson as well as the domain area goal, followed by small group work with computers and ending with a plenary in which the L2L2 goals are revisited.

The introduction to each lesson could contain:

- Explicit objectives for both the domain content of a lesson *and* the L2L2 goal, for example distributed leadership or mutual engagement or listening to each other and asking for reasons
- Revising the shared expectations for team work (see Lesson 1 below)
- Modelling some of the shared expectations such as being creative or giving reasons or taking the perspective of the other person.

The plenary could contain:

- Explicit reflection on the processes of learning together: what worked? What problems were there? What should we do about this next time?
- Evaluation of the success of the L2L2 objectives of the lesson.

Direct students' attention to both content and process

Students tend to respond to cues from the teachers as to what it is that they are supposed to be learning. If they are used to lessons that are about content in mathematics or science that needs to be learned for tests, then content is all that they will learn. But when L2L2 goals are explicit, during the students' group work, the teacher needs to respond to both content and process.

Promoting L2L2 in your class

The biggest influence on the way in which children talk together in a class is the way in which the teacher talks to them (see Part B, Reader, Chapter 1 on promoting dialogue in the classroom). Learning to learn together can also be modelled by the teacher. When a student asks a good question you could give an answer, or you could throw it open to the rest of the group or the class and ask what others think, ask them to give reasons for their answers, ask them to explore for any more alternatives that they may not have considered and then see if there is an agreement about the answer.

Modelling L2L2 means that:

- All have opportunities to contribute ideas
- Reasons are asked for and given
- Alternatives are considered
- Agreement is sought (but not imposed).

There is an *emotional aspect* to L2L2. It is important to foster an atmosphere in which people do not feel frightened to make mistakes and to ask for help. Teachers can model this by being positive about mistakes and showing how they are always learning opportunities. They can also model this by being honest when they make mistakes or do not know the answer, and by genuinely asking students for help.

Learning to learn together is about attitudes that team members take towards each other – listening with respect and learning together – but it is also about *communication*. Sometimes students might not find it easy to offer constructive criticism. It would be useful to model explicit language and techniques for this. Shift the focus from the individual to the task. Instead of 'You're wrong,' ask 'Are you sure that will work? What if we try it this way?' Model language that is positive and supportive while being critical. For example: 'I think that is a good approach and a great help but I would change one thing.'

It is a good idea to model explicit language for disagreeing, for asking for help, for giving help and for giving reasons.

'I disagree with y because of x'
'Can you explain what you mean?'

If there is a disagreement in the team then model trying to understand why the other person sees it in the way that they do and the kind of questions that would help unpack the source of the difference.

Teacher interventions

Teacher interventions can often stop the students thinking for themselves. Model asking all in the group for their views, asking them to explore alternatives, give reasons, etc.

Collaborative learning between classes with the Internet

Although the teaching of expectations for talking together and learning together face to face is an important preliminary to moving into collaborative learning over the Internet, these rules cannot simply be transferred to the new communication medium. An example of an initial 'trust'-type exercise to build up a relationship between two classes anywhere in the world, especially for younger children, is for each class to send 'Class Representatives' or mascots to one another. The purpose of the Class Representative (usually a toy animal) is to help give the two classes a shared focus and theme for their communications. It can be taken on class outings, which can then be described to the partner class. It can be given a 'voice' of its own in email communications. It can go to visit individual homes and say what happened there. It can report on the weather or seasonal festivals. It might even get homesick. It can support effective group talk. At the end of the agreed project time, Class Representatives are sent home.

Conferencing has the potential to extend the community of inquiry established in one classroom to other classrooms and other communities. However, the effectiveness of communities of inquiry depends on the shared expectations for communication that are followed within them.

Using email

Many of the considerations raised by conferencing also apply to the use of email. Email can be more than an exchange of information. It can be a conversation or a dialogue, and dialogues for learning in school settings require a shared purpose and shared ground rules (see Part B, Reader, Chapter 1). The implications of this can be illustrated by a brief email exchange between primary schools in the Netherlands reported by Van der Meij and Boersma (2002) and quoted in Wegerif and Dawes (2004). As we join them, two groups of four children in each school are struggling with the task of designing flying machines. They have one email-based lesson each week in which they read their email from the other group and respond; on alternate weeks they work on constructing their machines.

'Transcript extract (a): We have a tip for you' is an exchange sent in the second week of the project.

Transcript extract (a): We have a tip for you

> ***2nd email from Flying Four***
>
> Hi Flying Children
>
> You asked us how we construct our plane, which materials we are going to use and how we will let it fly.

We don't know yet how we will construct it, but we think we'll use kite-wood, plastic {trays} and maybe cloth. How we will let it fly we don't know yet.

We apologize for knowing so little. . . .

Friday march 19th we went to the library, where we found Dewey numbers 659.2, 640.5, 659.6

maybe you can do something with it. . . .

We have a question yet. Which materials do you have and how will you let it fly? . . . Will you say something about your plane the next time?

2nd email from Flying Children

Hello flying four

These are the answers to your questions.

We use triplex for the plane. We throw it in the air. We are going to stand on the climbing frame and throw it away.

We have a tip for you. You can go to a DIY store and ask for cast-away wood. . . .

Would you please mention some titles of books that you use. Because we don't understand that Dewey number at all.

3rd email from Flying Four

Hi flying children

Here are the titles and authors of the books you asked for:

book 1 : Airlines from the author H.j. Highland.

book 2: Inventors from the authors Struan Reid and Patricia Fara. . . .

Thanks also for your tip to visit a DIY store.

The children found these email exchanges extremely motivating. They read the incoming message and discussed what it meant before constructing a shared response. It is interesting to see how they manage, in just three emails, to negotiate rules of clear communication at a distance in order to share useful ideas on how to construct their aeroplanes. At their best, email exchanges can encourage such productive dialogue. Many of the broader aims of the ICT curriculum can be met in successful email exchanges including helping children to develop as independent and creative learners able to use the Internet to learn from and with others.

The IWB can be used to collaboratively generate and explore email texts in a whole-class (or small-group) context using the shared screen. Children can see that how they interact in direct collaboration is different to the indirect collaboration of the email interaction, and they can share their own understanding of these differences and the underlying rules.

Effective searching on the Web

The World Wide Web contains a vast amount of information and is still growing exponentially. Teachers have the responsibility of helping children to understand the nature of the information contained in web pages, how it is produced and why, and to gain an understanding of the benefits and pitfalls of using web-based information. In this way learners become autonomous and can make sensible decisions about the type and quality of information they access.

Problems for children using the Web reported by teachers include:

- Information may be inaccurate or inappropriate

- The initial aim of a search of the Web can easily be forgotten due to distracting; links; children sometimes lack a sense of what is relevant
- Left to themselves, even with clear guidance, children frequently conduct searches related to their leisure interests
- Unproductive searches are time-consuming and frustrating
- Children may confuse the finding and printing of information from the Web with acquiring knowledge or developing an understanding of the topic.

Working and reasoning together as a group can provide the support needed. An effective search of the Internet is essentially a reasoning exercise in which the searcher or group is faced with choices and asked to make decisions as to the best way to go on the available evidence. The distracted, unfocused and poorly prioritized searches which teachers report are often a product of the difficulties children encounter when asked to work as a group.

An associated problem is that teachers may have been encouraged to see their role in working with computers as different from, and less directive than, their usual teaching. The role of the teacher when ICT is integrated into classrooms is often described as that of 'facilitator'. Using computers in groups, children *can* be left to learn for themselves – but peer support, sensitive teacher intervention and the structure of L2L2 expectations help to enable joint construction of meaning. The crucial task for the teacher is to integrate computer-based talk activities with the larger ongoing conversations of the classroom. Through this process children working at the computer are still held within the ties and motivating force of a relationship with the teacher and with the class.

The IWB can play a key role in teaching children to use the Internet effectively. The teacher can model effective searching using the Internet live on the screen, and can facilitate a dialogue around interpreting the outcomes of searches, again using the language of reasoning. Web-based educational resources such as online videos, simulations and animations can also be played live and spontaneously according to the direction of a discussion. The IWB can also be used as a prompting tool – providing questions or multimedia to facilitate search alongside space to add information as the children find it.

Information can be found in books or on the Web; but in themselves texts and web pages do not *know* anything. Knowledge only exists when someone reads a book or web page and understands what is being said. Children seek to understand things for socially defined purposes as part of ongoing dialogues and relationships. What they find on the Internet must be brought into dialogues and integrated into the larger dialogue that is the construction of shared understanding in the classroom.

A key question which children can ask one another when engaged in Internet searches is, 'How does this information help with our shared purpose?' A useful activity for developing discrimination is to take a selection of websites offering information about the same topic and ask the children which they trust most and why. Using a shared display – such as an IWB – can facilitate this process. The aim of this sort of activity should not primarily be about the practical capabilities of conducting a search, although guidance may be needed here; instead, it could focus on encouraging children to reason together to find and evaluate information effectively. There are also many new web-based tools to help support students in learning to search the Web and to support teachers in setting exercises with searching (see Appendix B7.1 for links and descriptions). These tools are great but they do not replace the need to teach students how to think critically and challenge and develop the information they find on the Internet.

Conclusions

Computers, tablets and mobile phones provide an excellent focus for group work and for teaching the L2L2 skills that are needed in the Internet Age. Groups often seem to gather spontaneously around any new technology, trying to understand it and make it work. Teachers can harness such social learning opportunities both to help children learn within the curriculum and to develop skills for effective learning together with others. Computers can support the establishment of a community of inquiry among groups of teachers and learners. But without guidance group work can be too demanding and children can easily become distracted. Using the framework offered in this chapter of L2L2 with technology, teachers can lead students to take full advantage of the educational potential of the Internet.

References

Van der Meij, H. and Boersma, K. (2002) Email use in elementary school: an analysis of exchange patterns and content, *British Journal of Educational Technology,* 33(2): 189–200.

Wegerif, R. (2013) *Dialogic: Education for the Internet Age*. London and New York: Routledge.

Wegerif, R. and Dawes, L. (2004) *Thinking and Learning with ICT: Raising Achievement in Primary Classrooms*. London and New York: Routledge.

PART C

Resource bank

Dialogue and IWB activity descriptions with screenshots

All videos referred to can be found at http://tinyurl.com/OUPIWB

Note that all templates referenced are provided in SMART Notebook format and some are duplicated in ActivInspire, where indicated. Reader Appendices are in only the format originally provided by the teacher.

C1 Starting simple

Displaying an open-ended prompt and/or picture(s) to stimulate discussion in whole class or groups

Is it possible for us to imagine the experience of trench warfare?

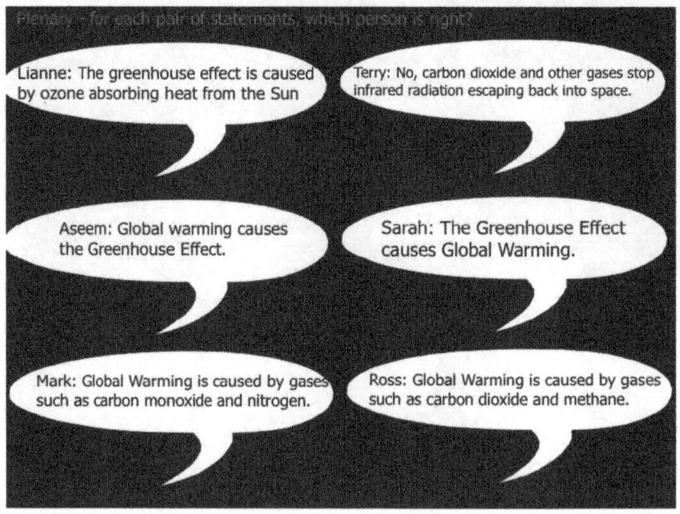

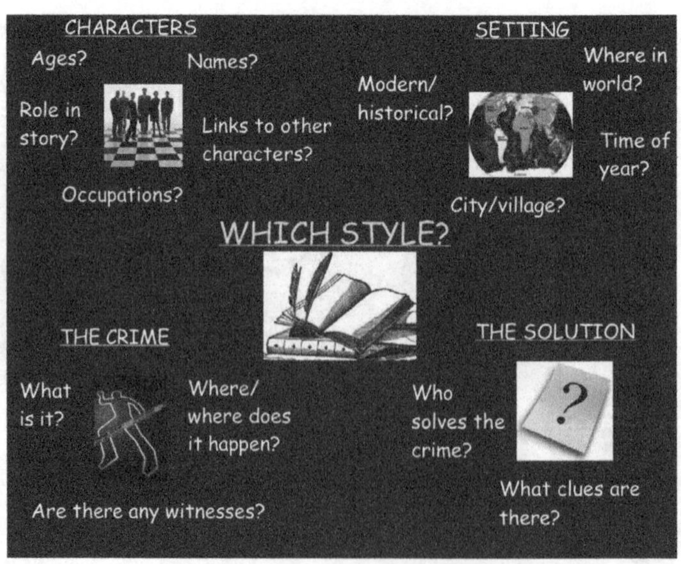

You might want to start by using the IWB as an ordinary whiteboard, simply using a text or picture stimulus to encourage and focus discussion. You might even start by asking a really general question such as 'Why is that on the screen?' or 'What do you think is happening here?' or 'What meaning could this image have for the lesson we are doing at the moment?'

Using images combined with text helps to enliven information, or illustrate/review key points and characters in a complex story. You can also flip quickly between screens to draw on a variety of evidence.

TIP: Images taken from the Internet, for example via a Google search, are almost always subject to copyright and you cannot reuse them without permission. To filter your Google search to images licensed as re-useable ('Creative Commons'), just enter the search term at http://tinyurl.com/googlecc1.

See templates: Notebook ideas – Photo stimulus; ActivInspire ideas – Photo stimulus
See flipcharts (for Examples 2–4): Reader Appendices B2.1, B3.1, B3.3

Class brainstorm

The teacher or students might exploit the interactivity of the board by using the pen to record ideas from the class in turn – underneath, over the top of or around the edges of the stimulus prompt or image, discussing each one. Saving the results could be useful later on too.

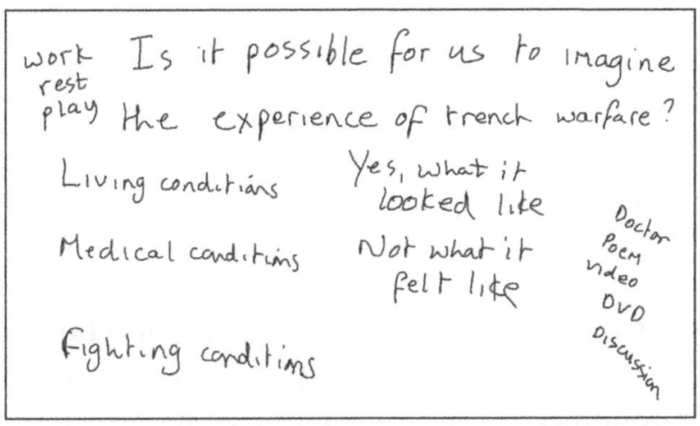

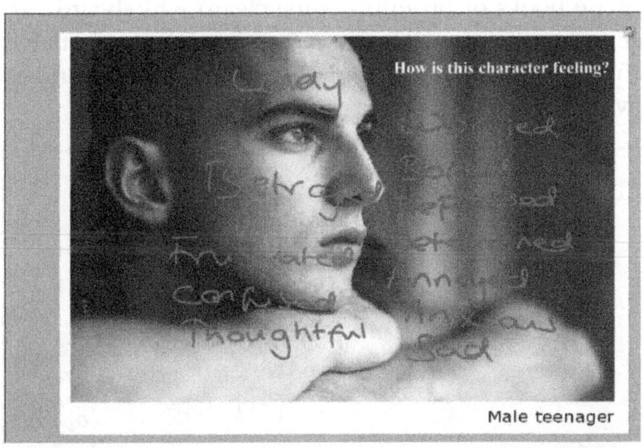

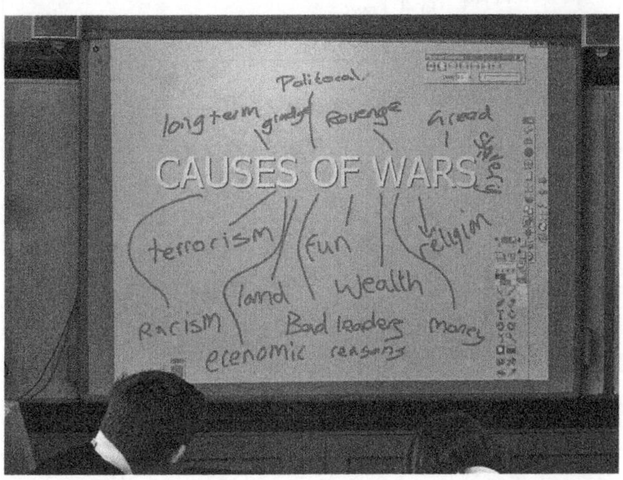

Video 8

Using pens to underline/circle key ideas

This is a very straightforward use again; teacher or students might underline key phrases or circle key elements using the IWB stylus ('pen'), explaining their rationale each time. In this example a student identified key phrases in an historical text (an army doctor's 1914 diary) while the teacher managed the discussion.

> If I ever get sent to the front with a regiment, I shall shed tears of joy. I do envy, Chris going off so soon but I think this dog will have his day soon too.
>
> We expect to be moved to the front at any moment. The men apparently will be in the trenches alternate 24 hours, changing with a fresh lot of men during the night. I am behind HQ, probably a dug out where I sit and wait for the wounded to be brought to me. I am told that doctors are not allowed in the trenches. I am told that the feeding at the front is splendid and there is a Daily Mail for every 10 men.
>
> Our men have had a terrible experience of 24 hours in trenches, drenched through and in some places knee deep in mud and water. To see them come out, line up and march off is almost terrible. They don't look like strong young men. They are muddied to the eyes. Their coats are plastered with mud and weigh an awful lot with the water that has soaked in. Their backs are bent and they stagger and totter along with the weight of their packs. Their faces are white and haggard and their faces glare out from mud. They look like wounded, sick, wild things. Many, too many who are quite beat are told they must walk it. Then comes the nightmare of a march of 2 to 4 miles which they do in a trance.

Students might also circle areas of an image for investigation and then verbalize their thinking.

Sharing, discussing and comparing ideas in a whole-class setting

Students can compare and contrast different perspectives by sharing them publicly using the IWB (writing or drawing) and talking them through. They might be primed for this by making notes or drawings of their ideas in exercise books or on mini- (wipe-clean) whiteboards, then share them with the class. In the first example from a history lesson, a pair of boys has negotiated a video storyboard and recorded their ideas on the IWB. The teacher can help students understand through the dialogue that there are often multiple, valid views.

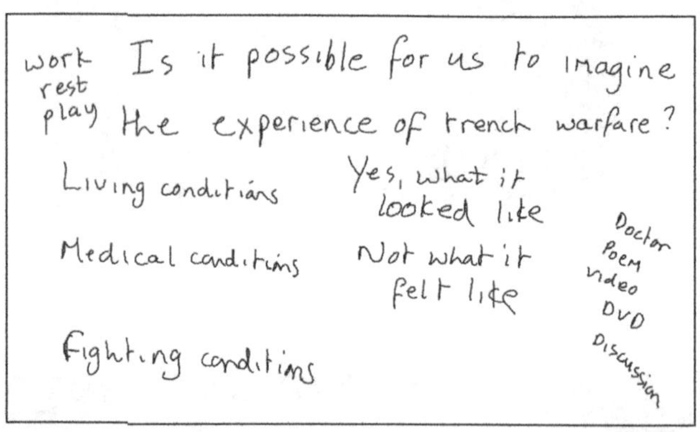

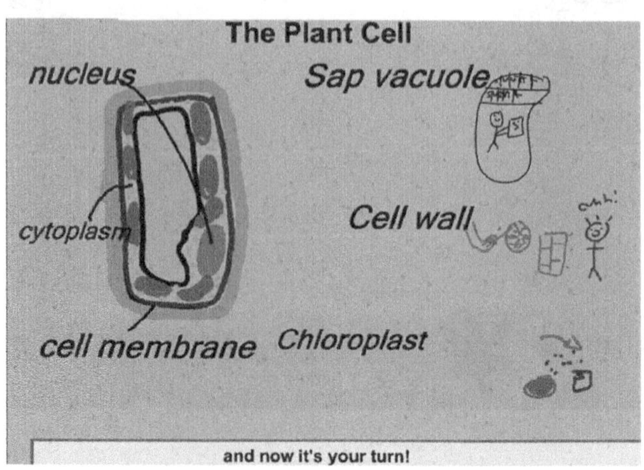

<u>How We See</u>

Susan and Steve made this drawing.
What do you think about their ideas?
You can change the drawing or the writing if you want to.

The light shines on the book.
I look at the book and see the book because the light is shining on it.

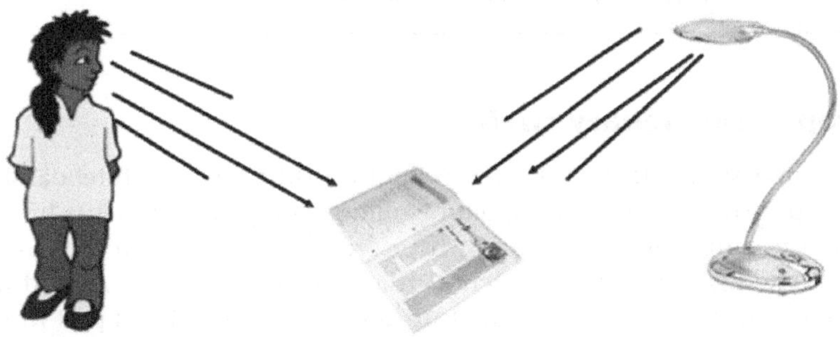

In the second example from science, students generated their own personal representations illustrating how the plant cell wall protects and supports. Some of these were then drawn freehand onto the IWB or projected there using a flexible camera (a form of visualizer) and publicly explained by students. In the picture shown, the cell wall protects a football player from a ball kicked towards him (the drawing adjacent to the words 'Cell wall').

Video 9

In the final example, students debate contrasting perspectives during a plenary session or perhaps in pairs/small groups during a lesson.

See templates: Notebook ideas – Annotating a diagram (a and b); ActivInspire ideas – Annotating a diagram (a and b)

Using 'AfL tasks' in developing dialogue

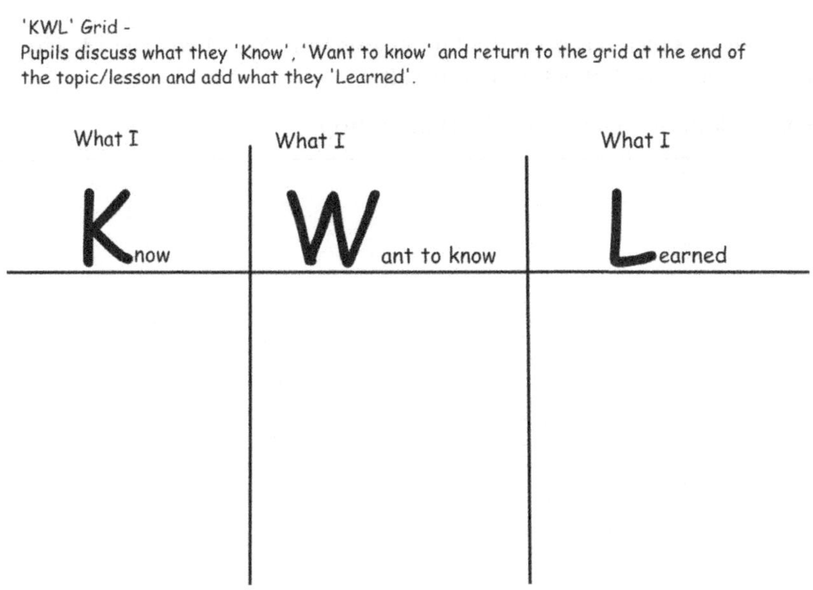

Many classroom tasks are explicitly designed to enable to children to articulate their understanding at specific points in their learning (Assessment for Learning); for example, 'concept cartoons' are often used in primary science classrooms to explore a range of ideas related to observable phenomena. Using an IWB for such collective tasks enables comments to be stored and returned to at different points in the teaching of a topic.

The template provided here is a KWL grid, where children are encouraged to express their initial *knowledge* about a topic and what they *want* to find out about it. There is then a space to review *learning* after a series of lessons.

See templates: Notebook ideas – KWL; ActivInspire ideas – KWL

Drag and drop – the plenary circle

This is adapted from a simple idea by Danny Nicholson (http://www.whiteboardblog.co.uk/2011/01/iwbs-8-ideas-to-keep-it-simple/) for finding out or summarizing what students have learned at the end of a lesson. It consists simply of a large circle, with words arranged around the outside. All students get thinking time to come up with several sentences that start 'I know that . . .' and then use one or two of the words in a sentence. Select a few students to come to the board and pull words into the circle to share their sentences with the rest of the class.

To make it dialogic, make the words more provocative and/or ask students to link their sentence to what the previous person has said, or to respond to what the previous person has said before they contribute their own sentence.

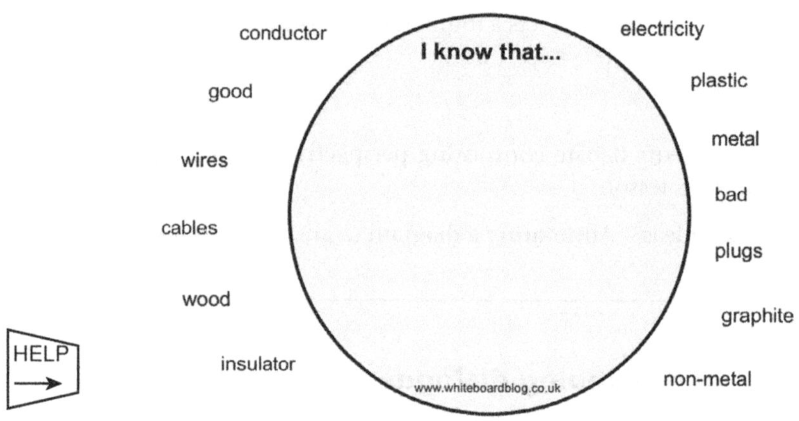

Danny reports that this idea has been used in lessons from Year 1 to Year 13. The idea is the same; it's just the words and concepts that get more difficult.

See templates: Notebook ideas – Plenary circle; Drag & drop

C2 Moving on

Highlighting and annotating texts or images: recording a teacher voiceover

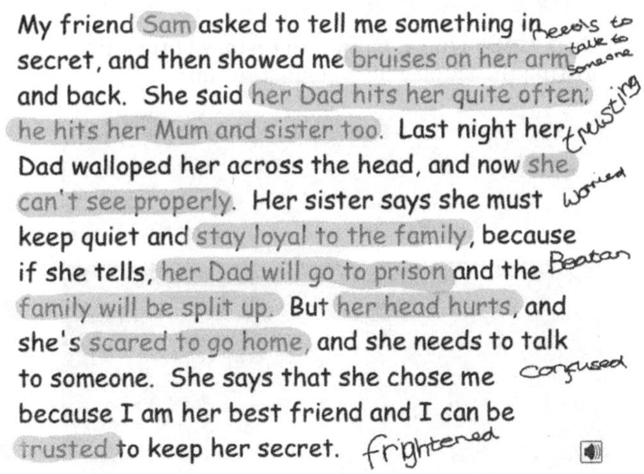

In **Video 10** we see Diane's use of a recorded version of on-screen text, where the teacher first played an audio file of herself reading out a personal safety scenario for children to discuss. This use of recording brings a different voice to the classroom, engages students and allows the teacher to focus on the students' reactions rather than on the act of reading.

Using the colour highlighter or annotating with the IWB pen can be particularly effective in drawing attention to particular aspects of a text, picture or other digital resource and in developing and recording interpretations of it. **Video 11** starts with the key parts of the text ('suggestions about what people think is really important') having previously been identified by the students and highlighted. Here, the students suggest words and phrases that may be useful in their coming group discussions about secrets. One student annotated around the text to represent a peer's understandings of the characters' feelings, with the teacher managing the discussion. We can see that students were stimulated to go beyond the printed text, generating and explaining their own ideas and illustrating empathy (e.g. 'beaten', 'confused').

Video 10

Video 11

Video 12 (Overall sequence)

See template: Notebook ideas – Recording sound
See file: Screen & Sound Recording (ActivInspire).pdf

Focusing attention using the spotlight, magnifier or 'cover and reveal'

You could use the 'blind' or 'cover and reveal' feature to create suspense and then reveal parts of a text or picture, or to reveal prompt questions one by one, to stimulate discussion.

You can also use the circular or rectangular spotlight feature to highlight selected parts of the screen.

Gas! GAS! Quick, boys! - An ecstasy of fumbling
Fitting the clumsy helmets just in time,

See templates: Notebook ideas – Rub to reveal; ActivInspire ideas – Rub to reveal

Understanding a text: taking it apart

You might use images related to a poem or other text to stimulate a brainstorm of students' own ideas and record these by annotating the text. In this way an original text can evolve into a richer resource. This example shows a sequence of IWB slides used during a lesson on the poem 'Education for Leisure' by Carol Ann Duffy. The originally projected text has 'disappeared' in the course of developing a dialogue exploring a character's feelings, the significance of an evocative image (second slide) for the poem's persona, and the ways in which the image and poem, plus other poems studied, reflect today's society. Capturing learners' interpretations is made easier through directly manipulating objects on the IWB, highlighting and annotating during discussion.

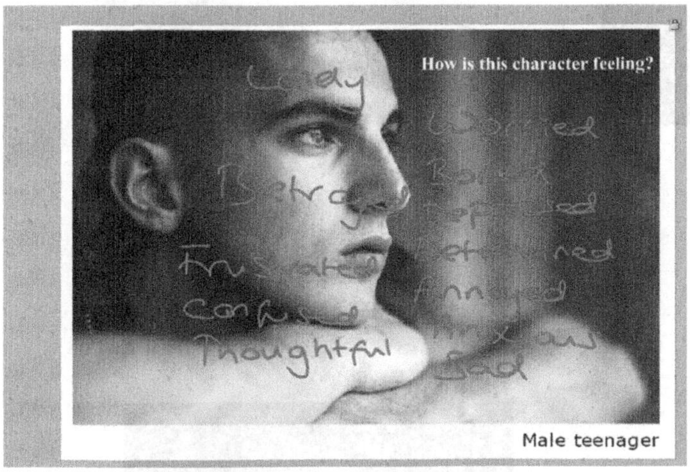

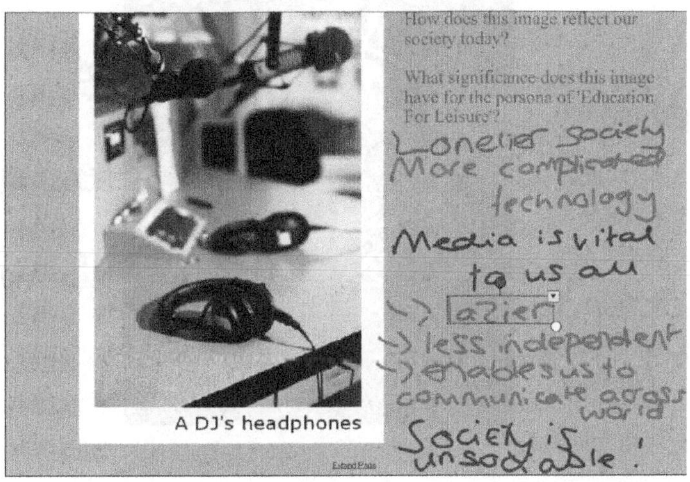

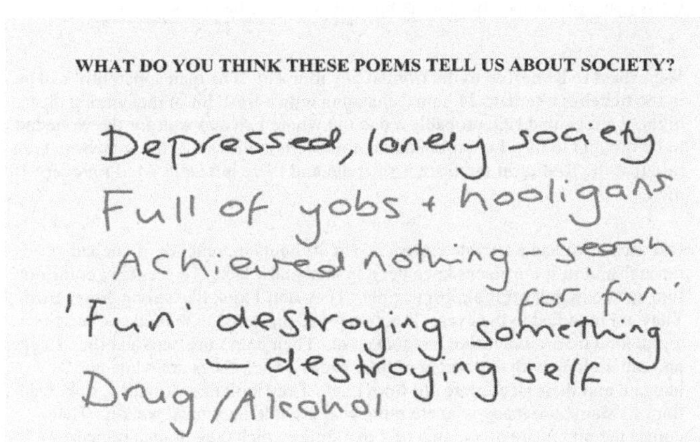

Getting students to build on each other's contributions; constructing knowledge together as a class

Students can be asked to come up in turn and move objects around to create a collective object that builds on previous contributions, as in this food chain example. Students each added a picture and a link in turn. Importantly, they were asked to explain their reasoning.

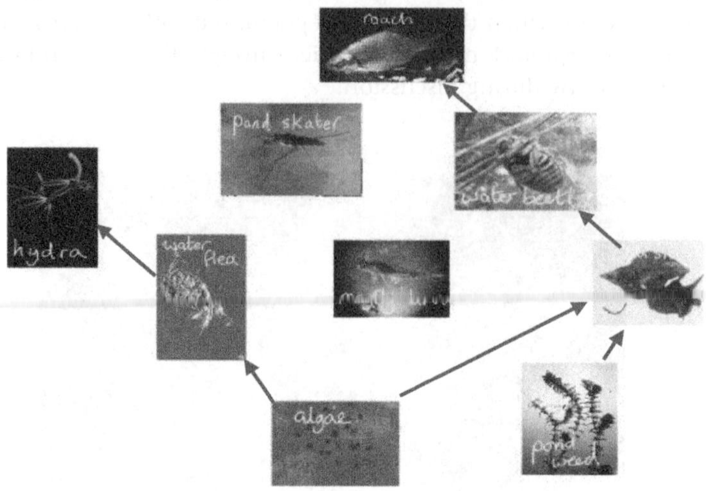

If I ever get sent to the front with a regiment, I shall shed tears of joy. I do envy Chris going off so soon but I think this dog will have his day soon too.

We expect to be moved to the front at any moment. The men apparently will be in the trenches alternate 24 hours, changing with a fresh lot of men during the night. I am behind HQ, probably a dug out where I sit and wait for the wounded to be brought to me. I am told that doctors are not allowed in the trenches. I am told that the feeding at the front is splendid and there is a Daily Mail for every 10 men.

Our men have had a terrible experience of 24 hours in trenches, drenched through and in some places knee deep in mud and water. To see them come out, line up and march off is almost terrible. They don't look like strong young men. They are muddied to the eyes. Their coats are plastered with mud and weigh an awful lot with the water that has soaked in. Their backs are bent and they stagger and totter along with the weight of their packs. Their faces are white and haggard and their faces glare out from mud. They look like wounded, sick, wild things. Many, too many who are quite beat are told they must walk it. Then comes the nightmare of a march of 2 to 4 miles which they do in a trance.

In the second example, students used the IWB pen in turn to record perceived characteristics of the young Queen Elizabeth I around a projected digital photograph of this historical portrait as shown. The work explored whether the 'Golden Age' of Elizabeth was truly golden! A second group of students subsequently interpreted their peers' thinking by drawing in links from their classmates' labels (written without comment) to features of the same portrait – they had to interpret someone else's thinking to do this. Finally, the teacher reflected with the class on the power of this collaborative enquiry and the scope of historical evidence offered by the paintings. Considering different perspectives and developing a more collective view of Elizabeth was powerful in altering their original individual conceptions although the teacher concluded that pictures only tell a partial story.

Video 3

In our third example of building in responsiveness to others' ideas, one student used the IWB underlining tool to identify key phrases in a historical text (an army doctor's 1914 diary), then the class were asked to explain his choices.

Video 5

Finally, students might be presented with part of a picture and asked to add the missing elements in turn. Note that in each of these examples, *getting students to respond to others' ideas is built into the activity.*

Drawing objects on the IWB together

As in the previous examples, students are building on each other's ideas here, and also on their knowledge and experiences from previous lessons. This time they are creating a joint picture by each adding an element in turn – this is a non-verbal kind of dialogue that creates a class product. Here the diagram depicted an imaginative range of elements perceived by students to be typically present in a trench, and it succinctly portrayed more than was said while drawing. It contained elements arising from the pair/class dialogue of their previous two lessons on trench warfare, 'building on their informed speculation from some of the things that they had seen' (teacher).

Video 13

Drag and drop, argue and explain

In these four examples from science, students drag and drop or sort the given images to show their understanding of a scientific process, and are then required to explain their reasoning.

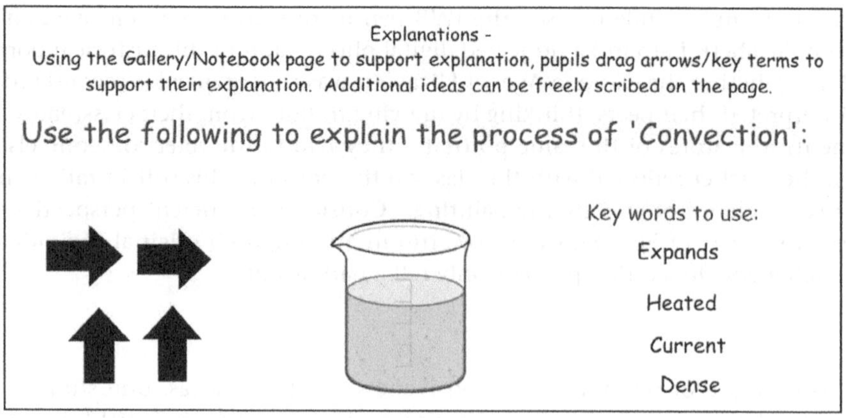
Explanations -
Using the Gallery/Notebook page to support explanation, pupils drag arrows/key terms to support their explanation. Additional ideas can be freely scribed on the page.
Use the following to explain the process of 'Convection':
Key words to use:
Expands
Heated
Current
Dense

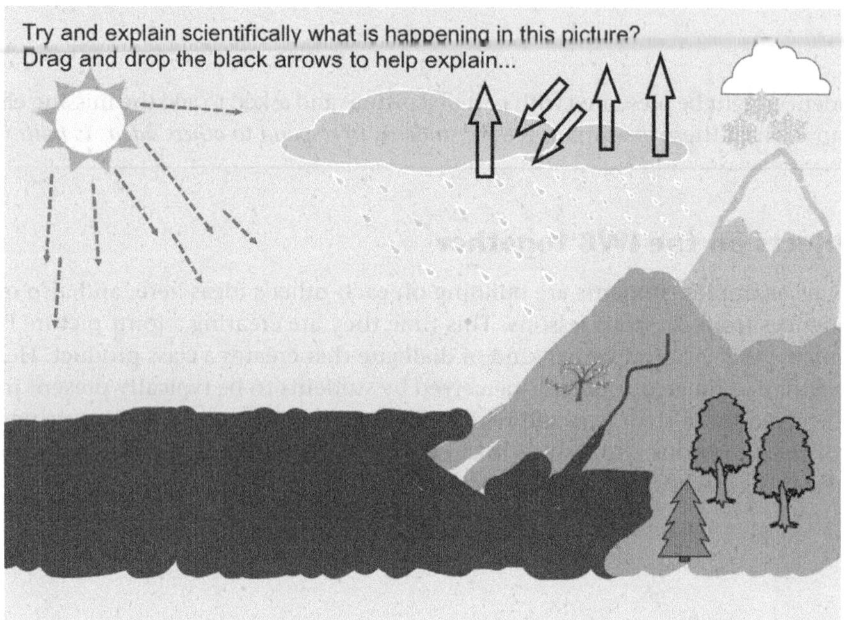
Try and explain scientifically what is happening in this picture?
Drag and drop the black arrows to help explain...

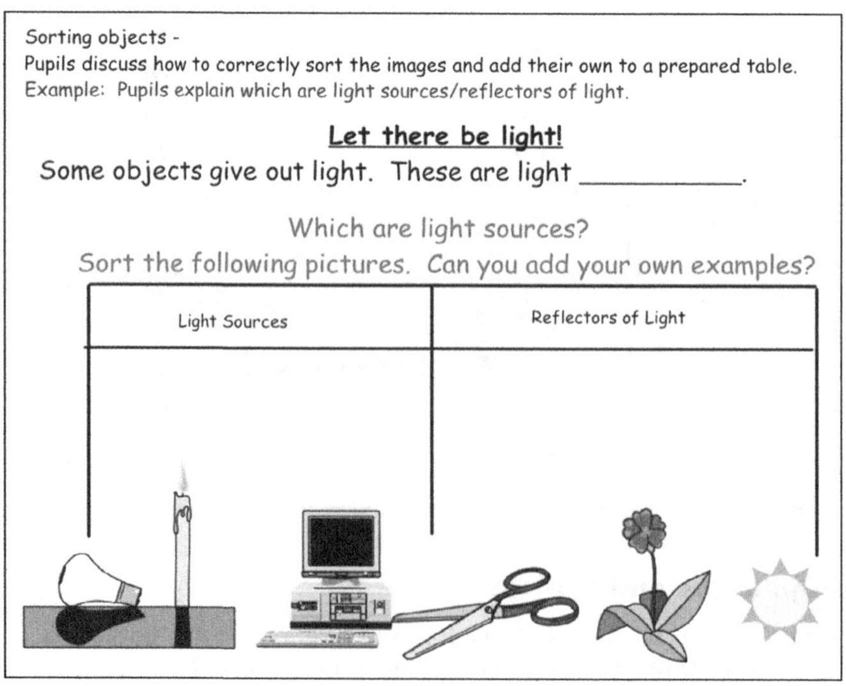
Sorting objects -
Pupils discuss how to correctly sort the images and add their own to a prepared table.
Example: Pupils explain which are light sources/reflectors of light.
Let there be light!
Some objects give out light. These are light ___________.
Which are light sources?
Sort the following pictures. Can you add your own examples?
Light Sources
Reflectors of Light

Drag and drop activity -
Use a series of images to stimulate discussion as pupils drag and drop images/shapes in place.

Example: Drag and drop the following to make a successful food chain.

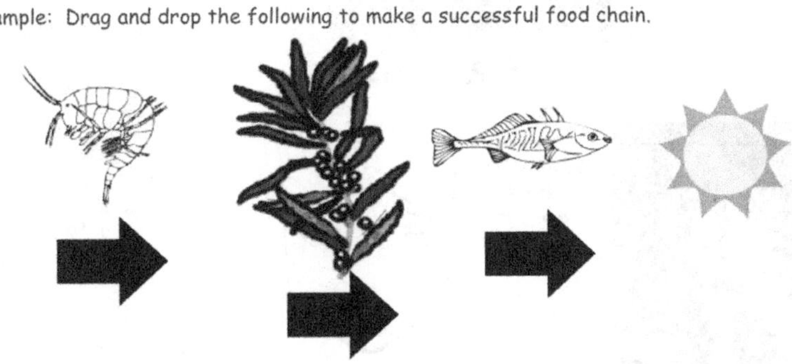

Drag and drop, argue and explain can also be used to sort theories or statements of fact, as in the mathematics example below: students place the statements in the chosen column and explain why they are true, false or 'iffy' (uncertain). (See also 'Square of truth' or 'magic box/window' activity below.)

True	Iffy	False	Don't know
A- The product of two numbers is a whole number	F- When you square a number the answer is positive	K- The sum of two numbers is greater than their difference	O- Dividing by a number less than one gives a larger number
B - Adding zero to a number multiplies it by 10	G- dividing by two then by 10 is the same as the opposite	L- Perfect squares have only 3 factors	P- Multiplying two numbers gives an answer bigger than either
C- The square root of a number is smaller than the number itself	H- two fifths of a number is the same as dividing by 5 then multiplying by 2	M- product of three whole numbers is never same as sum	Q- sum of two odd numbers can sometimes be odd
D- The product of two odd numbers is odd	I- Prime numbers are odd	N- The product of a positive and a negative is negative	R- The cube of a number is bigger than square
E- Square numbers have an odd number of factors	J- The sum of the digits of a multiple of 3 is divisible by 3		

See templates: Notebook ideas – Explanations (a and b); True/false/iffy (a and b)
See templates: ActivInspire ideas – Sorting objects; Drag and drop

Students selecting their own words/pictures/scenarios from a given set and manipulating/discussing them in pairs/groups

In the first example each group of four or five selected a slightly different combination of images pertaining to personal safety issues, arranged them on the IWB as they desired and annotated them during discussion (generating advice 'as a team working for Childline' and recording this on large sheets of paper). In the video clip one group talks through their ideas to the class, annotating the images; the teacher encourages other students to comment.

Video 15

One group outcome is shown. This can also be done with paper replicas at tables with one pair showing their work on the board afterwards, as in the second example from a science lesson (see 'Matched resources' below).

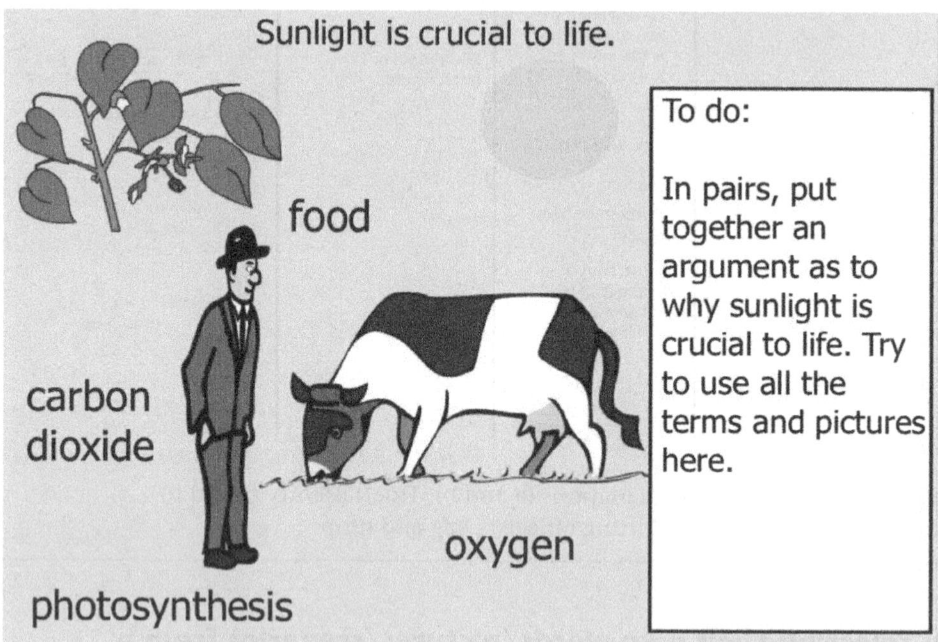

Image of 'divided loyalties' mask is reproduced by kind permission of the originator Wendy Morrell.

See flipchart (for first example) in Reader Appendix B2.2

Matched resources: students arranging objects on the board and at their desks

In this related example the teacher introduced the equation of photosynthesis using colour pictorial images of its components and an equation template on the IWB. The class were given paper mini-diagrams that replicated the IWB images (matched resources) and asked to cut up and order them, justifying their arrangements; this generated quite a lot of discussion and reportedly motivated students to 'want to know the answer'. The teacher circulated, talking to small groups of students, questioning and challenging their thinking. One student then came up to the IWB and moved the elements around to complete the equation. Students verified their own diagrams against this model before sticking the correct version in their books.

Video 14

This clip illustrates how the teacher used the equation on the IWB as an object of reference for the whole class, plus the mini-diagrams to stimulate thinking and support stepwise knowledge building; he continued this process throughout the whole sequence of lessons.

(For further diagram uses, see Clips 1.3, 2.3, 4.2, 5.1 on the T-MEDIA multimedia science resource at http://t-media.educ.cam.ac.uk.)

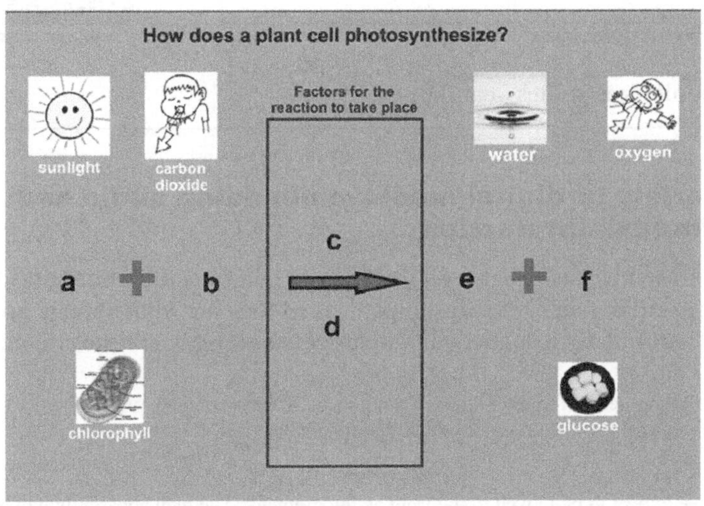

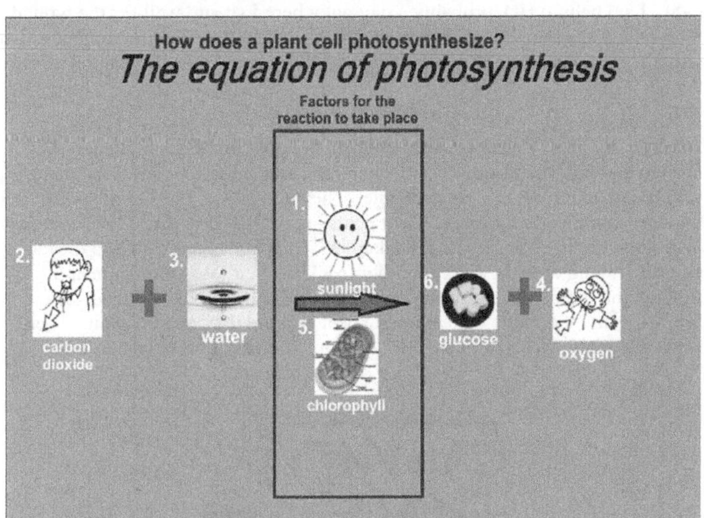

Discussing definitions: using hide-and-reveal tiles

Students can discuss the meaning of terms displayed on each tile, then clicking reveals the definitions underneath. They can add to or amend the definitions.

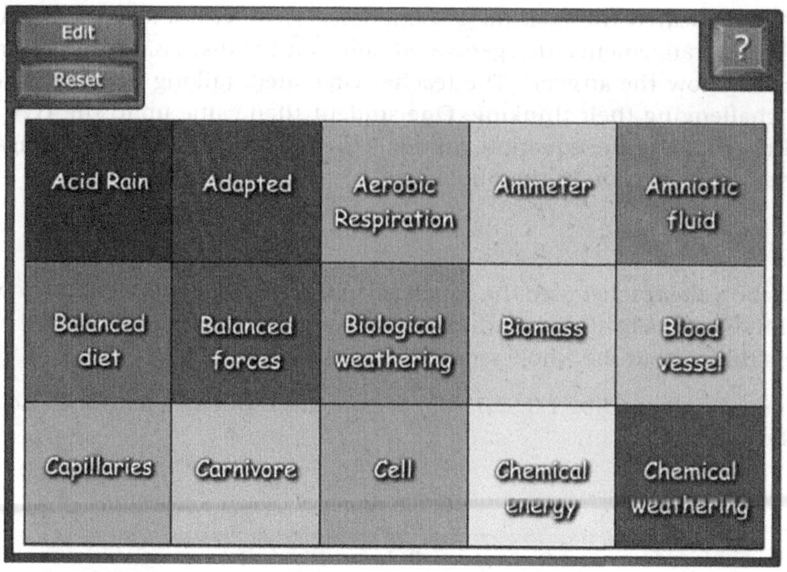

See templates: Notebook ideas – Tiles (a and b)

Using a wider variety of digital media: embedding audio and video for 'multimodal' interaction

You can use the IWB to switch easily between media or to combine different kinds from the wide range available – embedding audio, video, etc. into flipcharts so they are immediately accessible. This 'multimodal' use can help to stimulate dialogue, build up understanding over time and maintain engagement.

> If I ever get sent to the front with a regiment, I shall shed tears of joy. I do envy Chris going off so soon but I think this dog will have his day soon too.
>
> We expect to be moved to the front at any moment. The men apparently will be in the trenches alternate 24 hours, changing with a fresh lot of men during the night. I am behind HQ, probably a dug out where I sit and wait for the wounded to be brought to me. I am told that doctors are not allowed in the trenches. I am told that the feeding at the front is splendid and there is a Daily Mail for every 10 men.
>
> Our men have had a terrible experience of 24 hours in trenches, drenched through and in some places knee deep in mud and water. To see them come out, line up and march off is almost terrible. They don't look like strong young men. They are muddied to the eyes. Their coats are plastered with mud and weigh an awful lot with the water that has soaked in. Their backs are bent and they stagger and totter along with the weight of their packs. Their faces are white and haggard and their faces glare out from mud. They look like wounded, sick, wild things. Many, too many who are quite beat are told they must walk it. Then comes the nightmare of a march of 2 to 4 miles which they do in a trance.

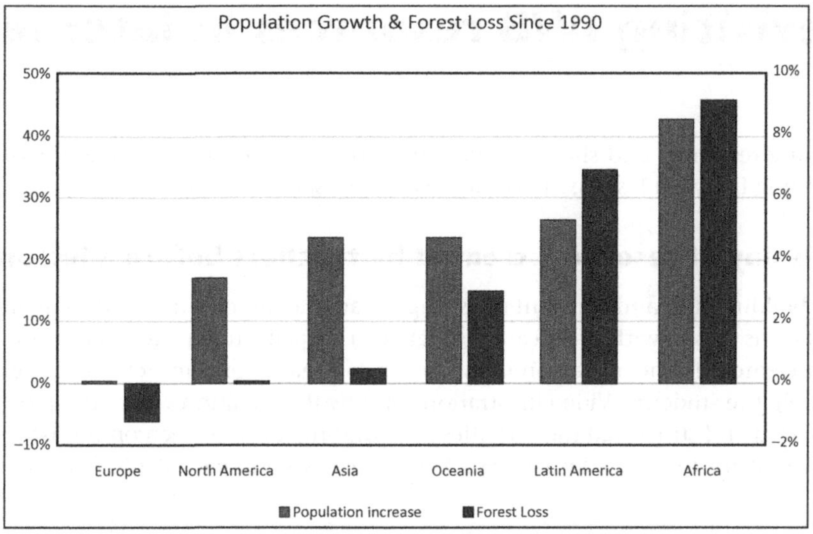

For example you might show a video to illustrate or analyse themes or texts. Apart from text, audio and video, digital resources include drawings, diagrams, still photographs, dynamic multimedia presentations, animations, simulations and models of dynamic processes, interactive diagrams or maps, databases, charts, graphs, tables, hyperlinked web pages, mathematical representations, musical performances, etc.

Combining lots of resources is illustrated in the lessons on trench warfare taught by Lloyd where a class explored the open-ended question: 'Can we imagine the experience of trench warfare?' The teacher employed a doctor's diary text, a poem, a YouTube video related to the poem, separate audio and video tracks of a single trench warfare film on DVD, a textbook trench diagram and wartime photographs; these conjured up different experiences and perspectives of life in the trenches.

Video 5 compilation

See template: Notebook ideas – Recording sound, Inserting video

See files: Screen & Sound Recording (ActivInspire).pdf [Templates folder] and Downloading, Inserting, and Embedding Video into ActivInspire [http://tinyurl.com/videoPromethean]

C3 Revisiting IWB resources in later lessons

Saving and reusing resources and slides is a very powerful way of building up and sustaining dialogue over time, including between lessons. This can be done in several ways.

Repeated display of resources created by teachers before a lesson sequence

The progressive building up – and constant revisiting of earlier components – of the equation of photosynthesis over six lessons (along with practical investigation) helped students to explore and understand the role of each core element in the overall process. The teacher made constant reference back to earlier learning in order to help the students. Video illustrations of how the equation was built up over time and how the teacher managed and structured the activities surrounding it can be seen on the T-MEDIA multimedia science resource at http://t-media.educ.cam.ac.uk (Clips 1.3, second part of 2.3, first part of 4.2, 5.1).

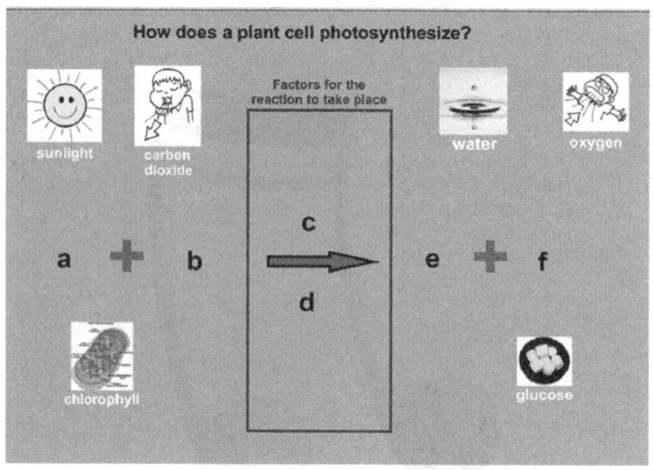

Revisiting objects that were annotated or constructed jointly by a class

This includes displaying previously annotated objects as optional, unobtrusive supports for further activity, such as students doing their own writing after studying a topic or piece of literature. It also includes allowing students to request or access resources or class products by themselves as needed for support.

One English teacher revisited the two annotated slides below in the subsequent lesson, to bridge between lessons, pulling together ideas from the two poems studied, and refocusing students, allowing them constant reference to their earlier ideas and thoughts. These memory aids reminded learners of what they already knew and provided a springboard for further discussion of the themes depicted.

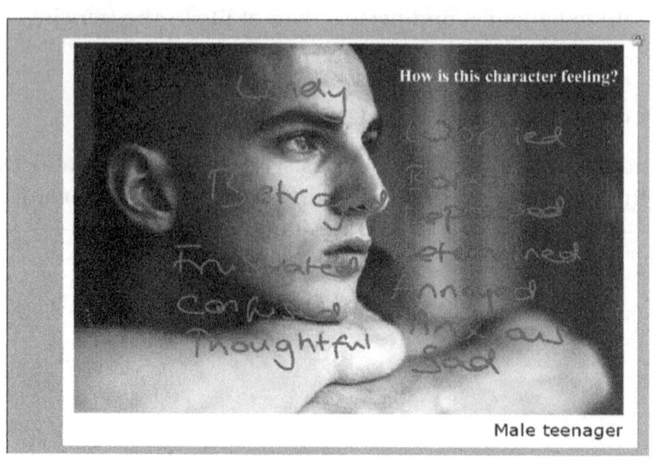

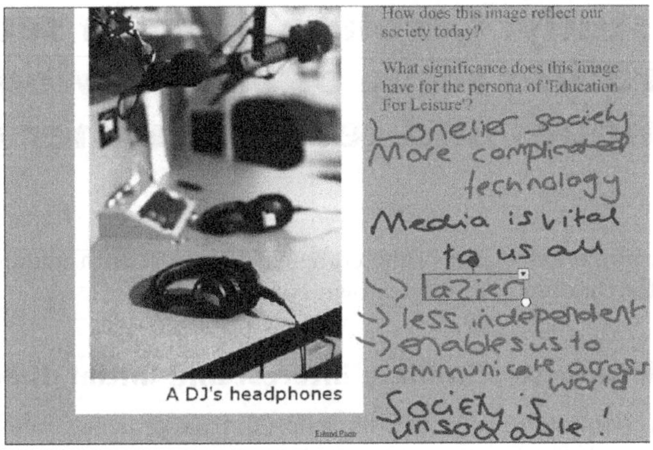

Revisiting objects created by other classes

Other classes' creations might be revisited as a memory aid, either as a stimulus to provoke thinking and make explicit learners' own views in response, or to explore differences between perspectives across and within groups. For example, history teacher Lloyd displayed a spider diagram depicting a brainstorm from another class about 'how wars start' for comparison and contrast with current conceptions.

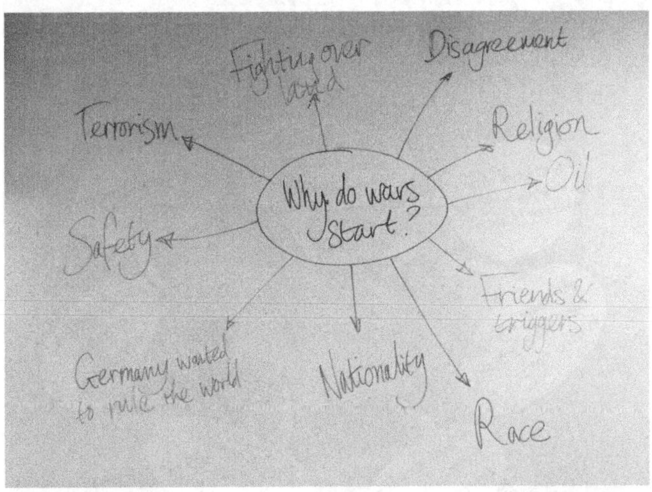

C4 Case study: Caroline's lesson sequence illustrating some of the previous techniques and several further ones

A series of lessons focusing on elements of the crime-writing genre with middle school children aged 12–13, in preparation for children writing their own crime stories.

Using text and pictures to stimulate interest and initial dialogue

Here we present a starter activity to stimulate discussion in pairs or table groups. The children have to negotiate a response to each item and consider the links between them. Note that a sound file – the 'Pink Panther' theme – is embedded in the picture. The slide was up at the start of the lesson and the music attracted the children's attention as they entered the room.

Clip illustrates teacher modelling responses and encouraging the children to consider alternatives.

Video 16

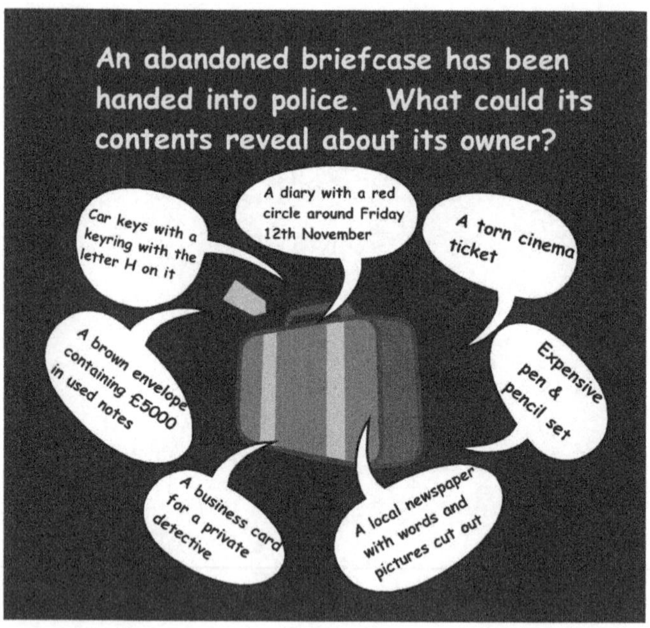

See flipchart: Reader Appendix B3.1

Matching terms and definitions

In a review of vocabulary from the previous lesson, explanations are moved by the children to match terms, confirming the accumulated 'common knowledge' from the previous lesson.

The clip illustrates a child getting the meaning of 'alibi' correct. It was important for this child, who misunderstood the meaning of alibi in the first lesson, to have the opportunity for dialogue with his group prior to completing this task.

Video 17

The second example of matching terms and definitions is from a science lesson. *(See also the related activity 'Interactive multiple choice quiz' in 'C7 Further Ideas', below.)*

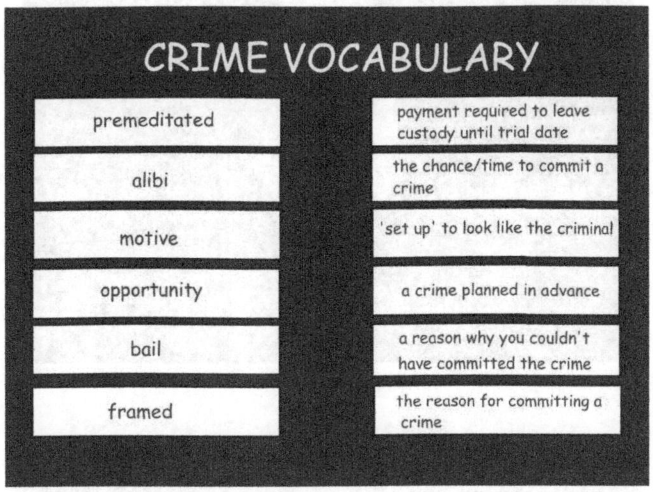

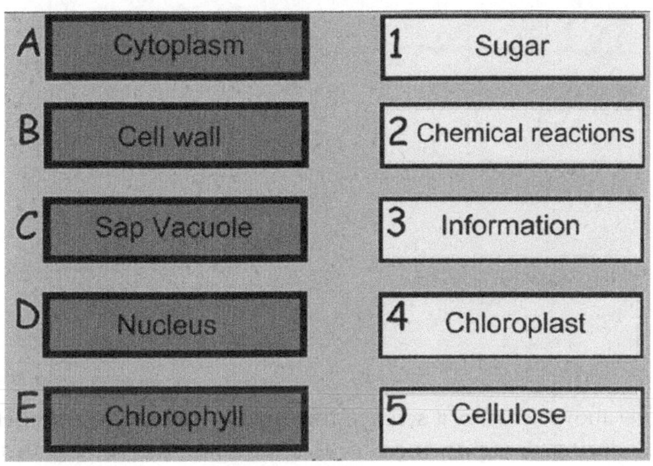

See templates: Notebook ideas – Word definitions (a, b, c)

'Square of truth' or 'magic box/window' activity

This activity creates suspense and stimulates discussion by allowing the teacher or learners to sort objects, words or text phrases according to their properties. For example, correct answers to a question, True/False, prime numbers, metaphors or addictive substances will be correctly categorized when dropped into the box (or other shape) or a window is dragged over them. Typically students are asked in turn to predict whether – and to explain why – a set of given statements will be true/false or fit the given category, then to drag the statements over a central square or other opaque object (a badge in the first, crime writing example) to receive immediate physical feedback about correctness. Statements deemed false by the teacher are previously formatted to disappear behind the box using the object layering feature of the proprietary IWB software; those that are true stay visible. This kind of activity can either develop or test students' understanding. In the first example, the aim was to consolidate children's understanding of the plot of a real-life crime, developing both crime vocabulary and ideas for their own crime story.

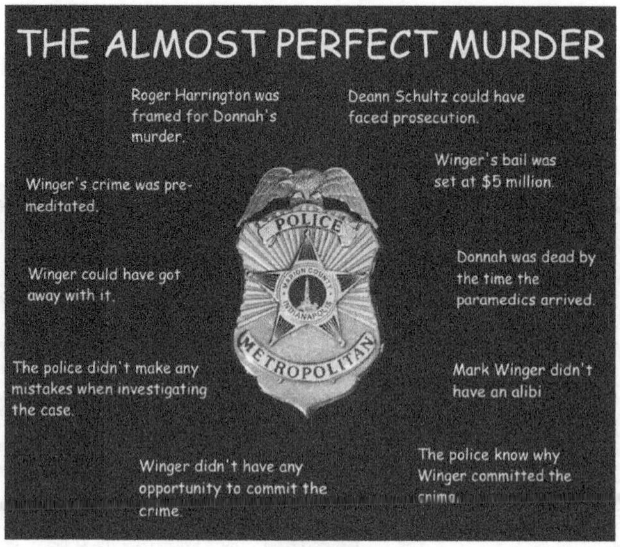

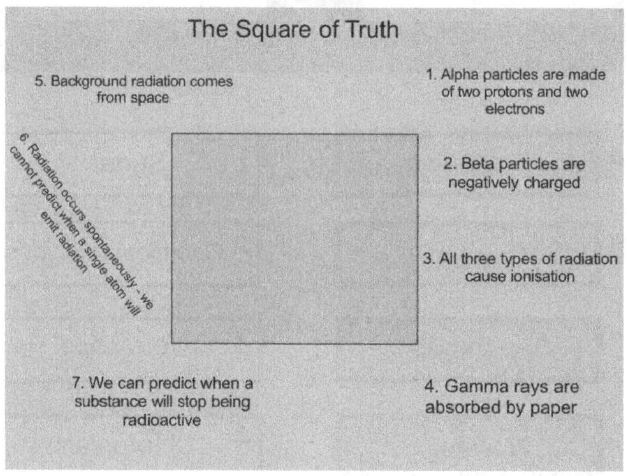

The second example above is from a science lesson. The third example below shows the objects (statements) before and during dragging them onto the object (the moon in this case). In the final example, Guess the shape or 'Box of truth', students might discuss and predict what shape they think is behind the box based on whether the clues are shown to be true (when dragged are on top of the box) or false (when dragged behind the box). The green box can then be moved to reveal the mystery shape.

Before manipulation

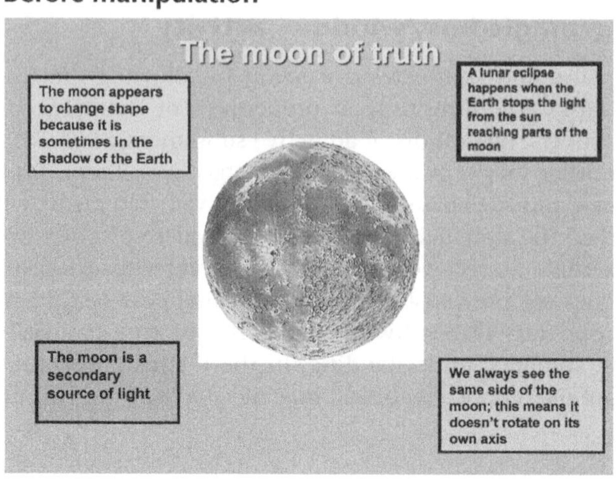

During manipulation

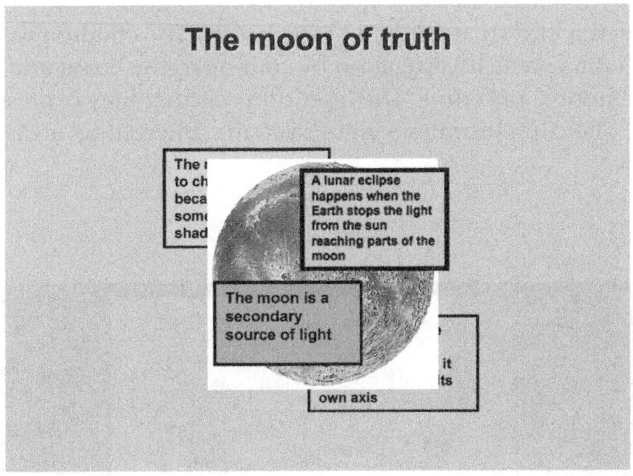

After manipulation

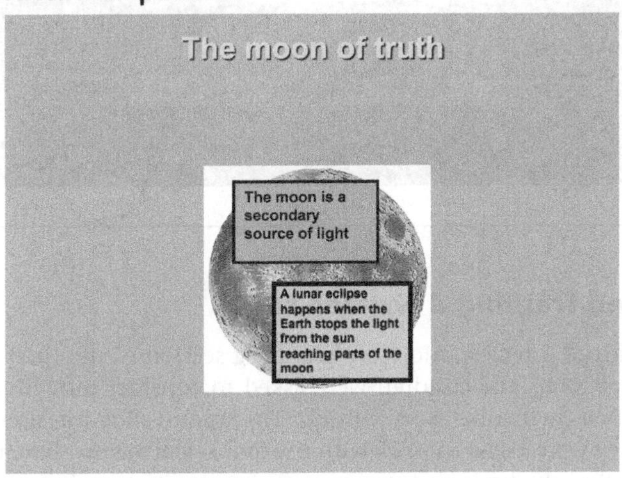

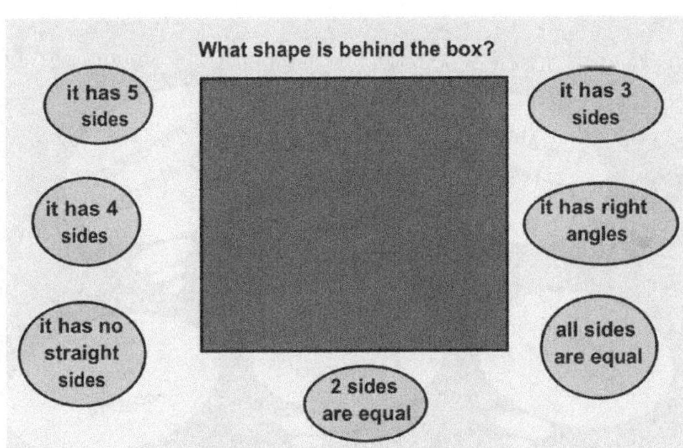

See templates: Notebook ideas – Magic window intro [instructions]; Moon of truth; Box of truth (a and b); Tortoise of truth (a and b)

See templates: ActivInspire ideas – Magic window intro [instructions]; Box of truth (a and b); Tortoise of truth (a and b)

Focusing on evidence – identifying key parts of the screen

The slide of a crime scene was shown at the end of the lesson. The children were asked to demonstrate their understanding of a crime scene investigation by coming to the board and circling anything in the scene that could help them solve the crime. The intention was that they express their individual understanding of these points. The clip illustrates a child selecting 'interesting' areas of the screen and being asked to explain his choice.

Video 18

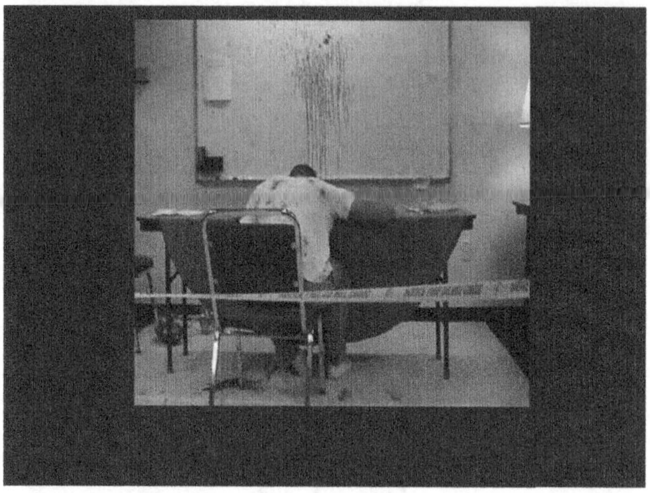

Reviewing work and framing a written task

These two slides were part of a review and story-planning section of the final lesson in the sequence. With reference to the first slide, the children were asked to consider individually how their previous work might impact on their own crime story writing. The second slide was used once the children had planned their stories. They were asked to work with a response partner to share their ideas; the response partner's job was to question the basis and structure of the plan to help improve it. The slide provided question prompts to help to maintain a focused dialogue.

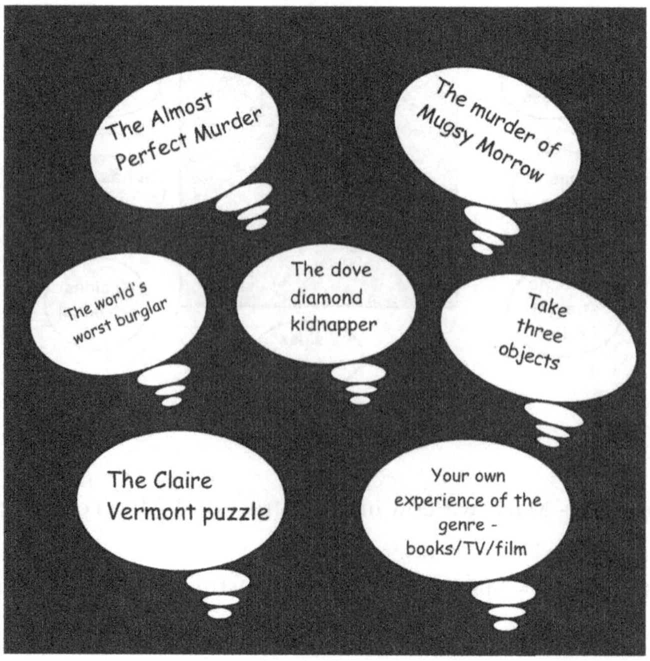

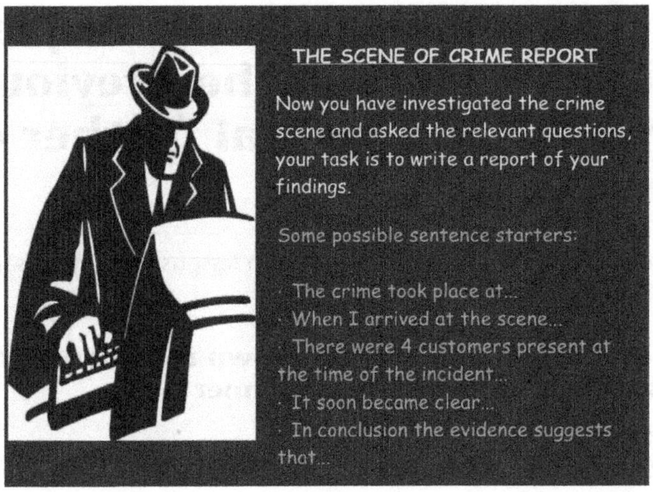

See flipcharts: Reader Appendices B3.2, B3.3

C5 Case study: Diane's lesson sequence illustrating some of the previous techniques and several further ones

A series of Personal, Social, Health & Citizenship Education lessons on 'staying safe' with primary school children aged 10–11

Using open-ended prompts and students' own recorded voices to stimulate discussion; use of ticker-tape/banner

(Use for Activity 3 of CPD Resource)
This clip is an introduction to the whole issue of keeping secrets. Diane uses a single image to stimulate some initial discussion, with a ticker-tape 'core' question dynamically streaming across the screen. She then uses sound files, recorded by children themselves before the lesson, to give the children 'another voice' through which they can express their ideas and which can then act as a stimulus for continuing dialogue. This is another way of sharing views orally. It is easiest to do using the IWB's own audio recording facility – even young primary children can operate this themselves – but can be done using a portable digital audio recorder too. Playing pre-recordings of students' opinions is an effective stimulus for class dialogue – it pre-packages the information for discussion; gives students more time to think about their responses than during a class discussion; opens up a space for students who might normally be shy to speak out in front of the class and encourages students to respond to each other. Audio files can be embedded in the flipchart so they can easily be clicked on to play in succession.

Video 4

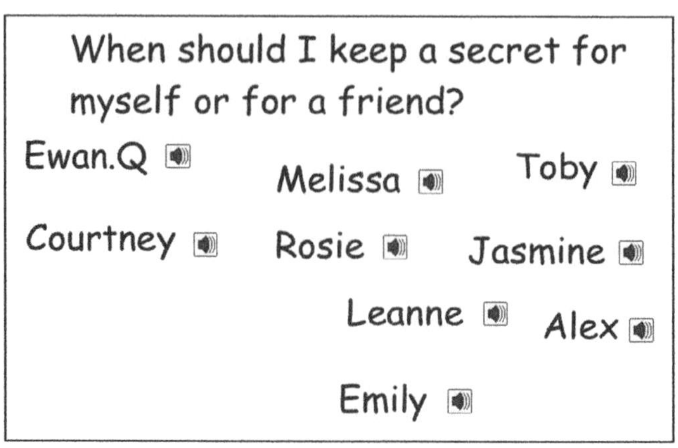

See templates: Notebook ideas – Scrolling banner (a, b and c); Recording sound
See templates: ActivInspire ideas – Scrolling banner (a, b and c); Recording sound
See flipchart: Reader Appendix B2.1

Group recording and explanation

This clip sees Diane picking up on work carried out in the previous lesson, where one group were asked to work at the IWB, annotating images with their initial thoughts about keeping secrets. One child tells the rest of the class what their responses were and Diane picks up on some key issues that are to be used in subsequent discussion. Thus the group dialogue from the previous lesson is continued over time.

Video 19

See the longer follow-up clip 'Choosing, annotating and discussing images related to personal safety on the interactive whiteboard' from later in the lesson (**Video 15**).

Image of 'divided loyalties' mask is reproduced by kind permission of the originator Wendy Morrell.

See templates: Notebook ideas – Cartoon strip (a and b); Explanation (a and b)
See templates: ActivInspire ideas – Cartoon strip (a and b); Explanation (a and b)
See flipchart: Reader Appendix 2.1

Negotiating classroom rules and procedures using the interactive whiteboard

While this clip illustrates a simple use of the IWB by a child in the class, its main purpose is to illustrate the idea that in order for children to talk productively they need to know how. Here the teacher introduces some talk rules for the students to trial and provides an opportunity for them to discuss which they see as important. The aim is to support classroom dialogue in the activities that follow.

Video 1

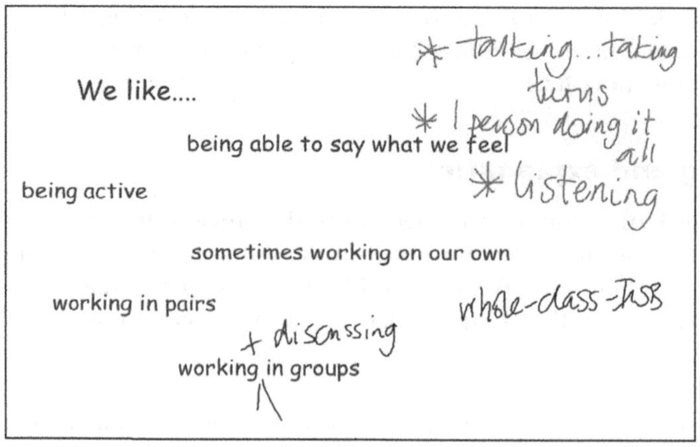

See flipchart: Reader Appendix 2.2

Working using class talk rules

The IWB slide presents a scenario for students to discuss in groups. There are some prompt questions that follow on the slide, which were the basis of some whole-class discussion before the group work. The clip shows one group using talk rules to explore the scenario.

Video 2

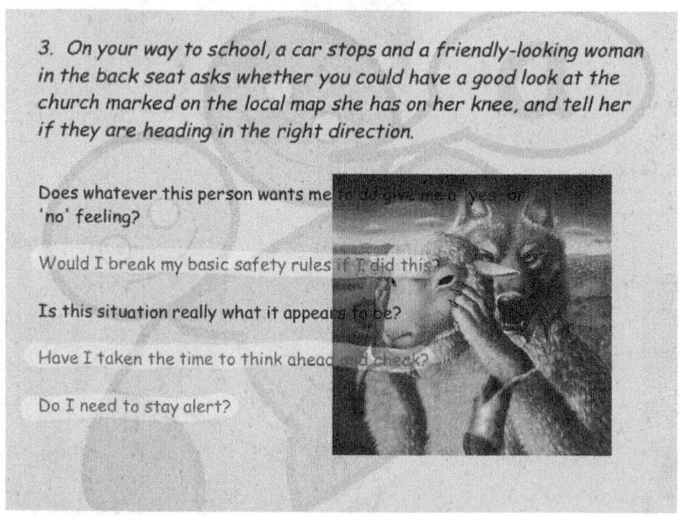

See templates: Notebook ideas – Dice roll (a and b)

C6 Students working semi-autonomously in groups at the IWB

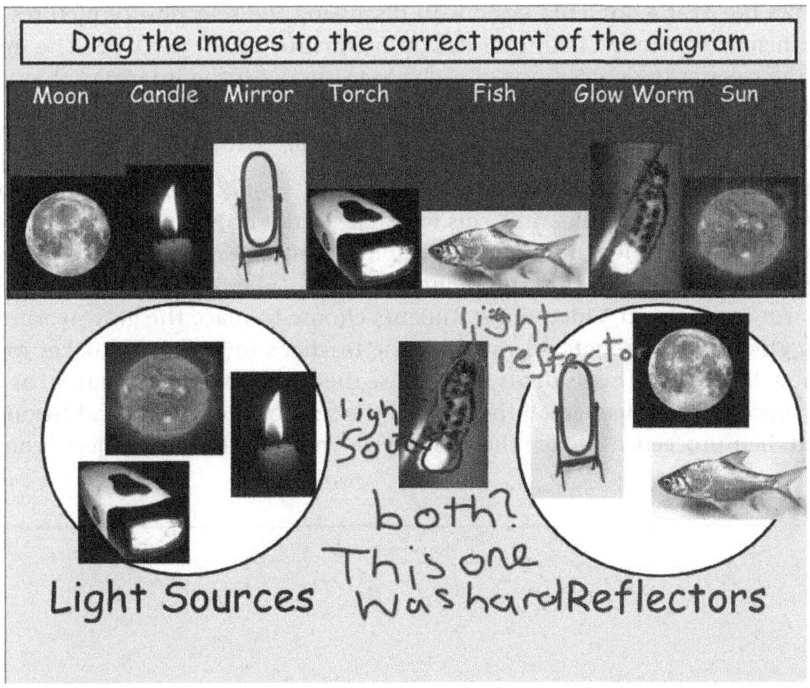

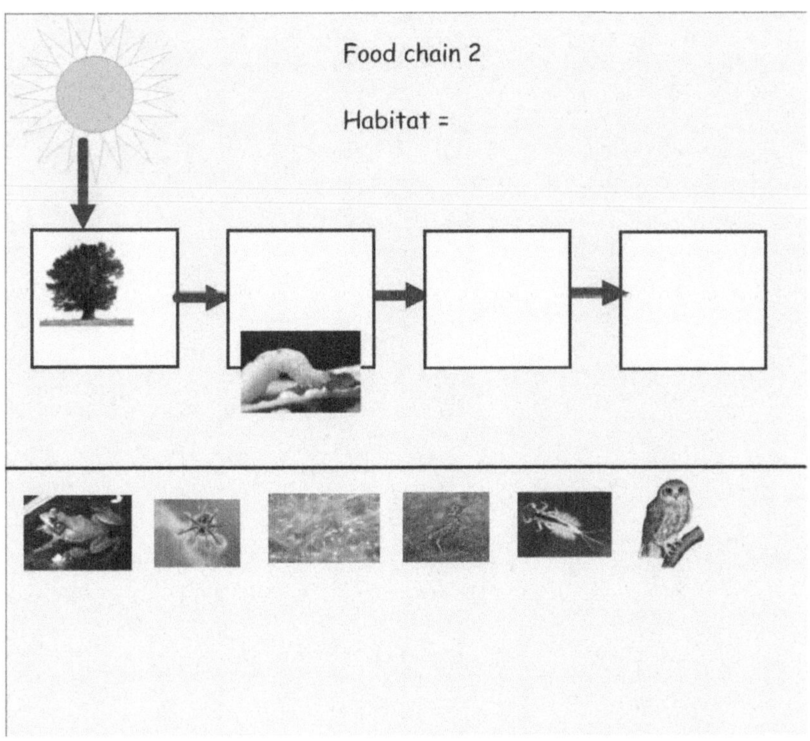

Two video clips illustrate primary school students in groups using the IWB semi-autonomously; these are **Videos 6 and 7**.

The IWB environments that feature in these lessons have both been set up by the teacher to have some elements that are fixed and some that can be moved by the students. Thus, the students' choices with respect to reconfiguring the IWB screen are restricted, focusing them on the specific intended learning for the task.

Video 6 shows three students from a Year 5 class (aged 9–10) engaged in dialogue about where to place a glow-worm in a categorization of objects as light sources or reflectors. In this example, the page sorter is open and provides easily accessible links to other tasks in the same topic. In this way the whole IWB file for the lesson can act as an assistive memory device for the pupils, should they need it.

Video 7 shows the Year 4 students (aged 8–9) discussing the selection of pictures of living things prior to placing them into a food chain that has been constructed on the IWB. The images have been hyperlinked by the teacher to descriptions of each organism, with the intention that the students can access information relevant to their task at appropriate times.

The key issues in setting up such IWB environments for students are:

1. How many elements should be fixed and how many should be open to movement, hyperlinking or adaptation by the students? This will depend not only on the age and experience of the students, but also on the nature of and complexity of the task.
2. How open to interpretation are the elements that are adaptable by the students, and does this matter? For example, in **Video 6** the students choose to place the glow-worm in the centre of the two groups and, though this was not the teacher's intention, it makes for a much richer discussion. In **Video 7** the students did not use the hyperlinked information as intended by the teacher; instead, they opened all the links at the start of the lesson, read through the information and then proceeded (hence their irritation when touching an object brought up a hyperlink).

C7 Further ideas

Model mapping/mind mapping

Students use key terms and drag and drop words/draw arrows/add text to make connections and explain key ideas about a topic. Results can be saved and added to throughout a lesson/topic of work. Learners could make a mind map at their desks before or during the class activity, or they could do the activity at the beginning and end of a lesson or lesson sequence to illustrate to themselves and the teacher what they have learned. This is especially useful for children with literacy difficulties.

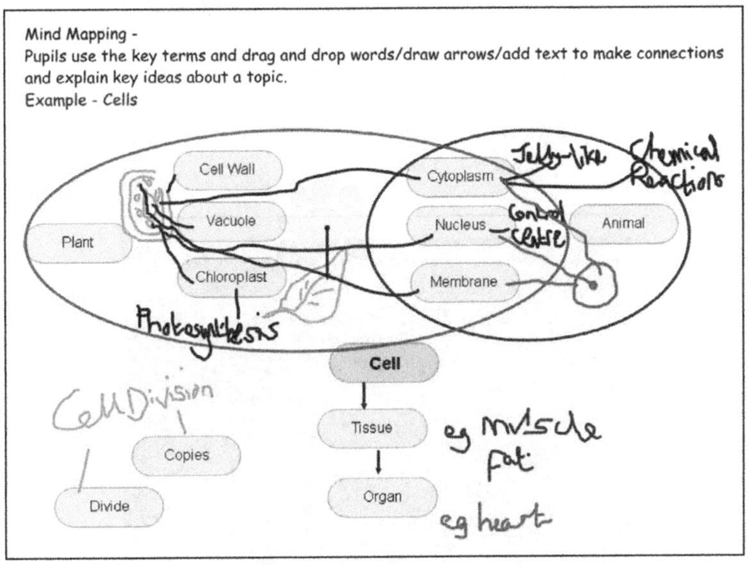

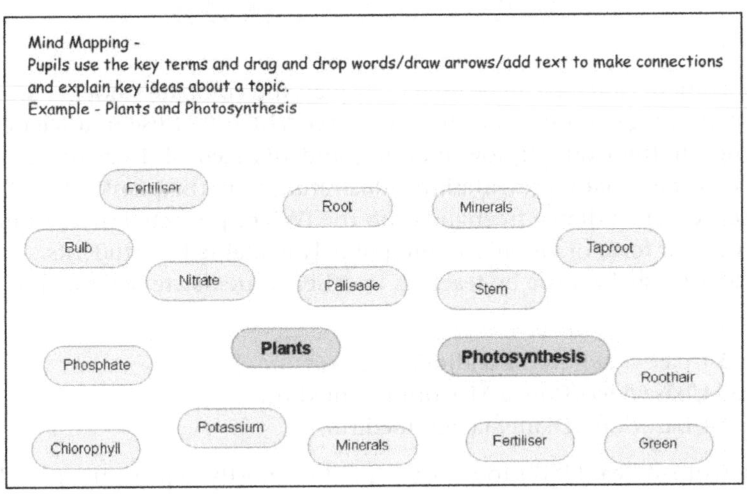

See templates: Notebook ideas – mind map (a and b); ActivInspire ideas – mind map (a and b)

Generating and testing provisional ideas

Teachers can support trialling of ideas and create joint responsibility for learning through encouraging students to make *conjectures*, non-verbally using the IWB as well as verbally. The teacher supports student understanding by providing or requesting further explanation or clarification. Other students can join in, especially when someone at the board seems uncertain.

Examples we have already seen include in this Resource Bank: playback of children's own audio recordings of opinions about personal safety as stimuli for class discussion; students in turn contributing links to a food chain; and students testing out conjectures using a 'magic box' or 'square of truth'.

Use of a visualizer with the IWB

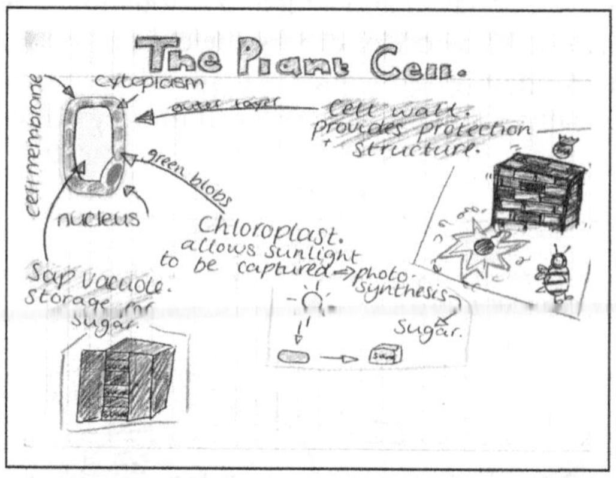

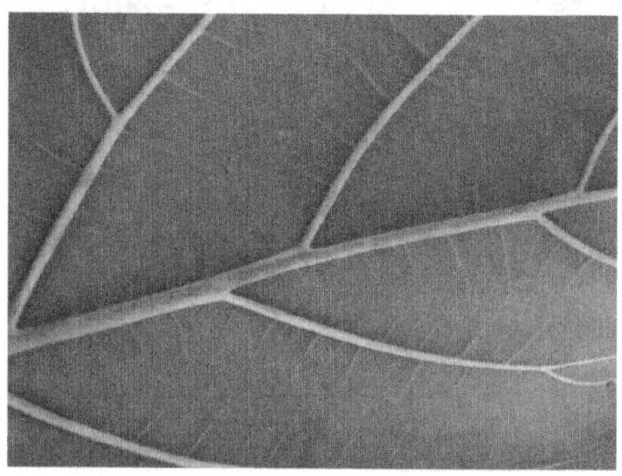

The visualizer (or document camera) can be used to display and compare students' work or experimental results, or to project an image as a stimulus for a task. See **Video 9** of use in a science lesson at (play it from 41.05 to the end). In this example, low attaining students aged 14–15 learning about photosynthesis generated their own personal representations illustrating how the plant cell wall protects and supports. Some of these were then drawn freehand onto the IWB or projected there from their books using a flexible camera (iCam or form of visualizer) and publicly explained by students.

Further examples of visualizer use by teachers in other contexts are described in these videoed presentations:

rtsp://svl.ioe.ac.uk:554/basevideo/StevenandJulie_med.rm
rtsp://svl.ioe.ac.uk:554/basevideo/DougalMcCormick_med.rm
rtsp://svl.ioe.ac.uk:554/basevideo/DianeMavers_med.rm

You may need to download Real Player to view them. They mostly depict primary school uses but they will give you an idea of the tool's versatility. They include rolling a dice for a class to see, showing equipment (ruler/protractor/syringe), scrutinizing the structure of bread going mouldy, projecting children's work and a photostory. You can also freeze an image, then remove the object from the visualizer and manipulate it, and compare it with the original.

Interactive multiple choice quiz ('Who wants to be a millionaire?' style) or drag-and-drop matching activity/vortex sorting activity

This is closely related to the activity 'Matching terms and definitions' in Caroline's lesson sequence, where students drag explanations/statements to match key terms. You may do these kinds of activities to review the meanings of terms or students' understanding of a topic area or process (soliciting their own everyday knowledge or what they learned in a previous lesson).

Word definitions - In this example pupils might discuss and match-up the description to the key word. Following discussion, definitions can then be added to/amended or deleted and re-worded.

This can be found in Gallery, Lesson Activity Toolkit 1.0, Activities, Keyword match

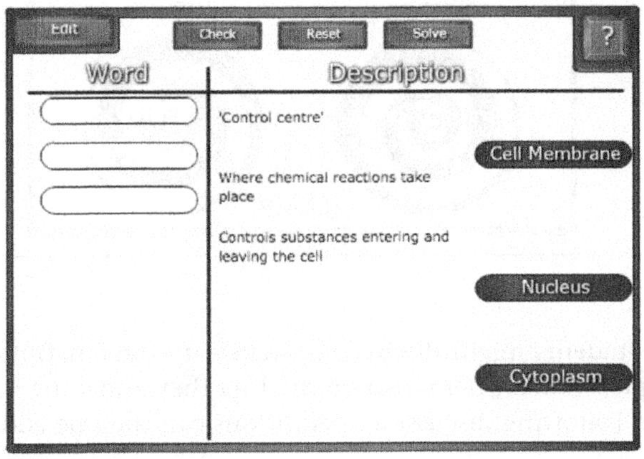

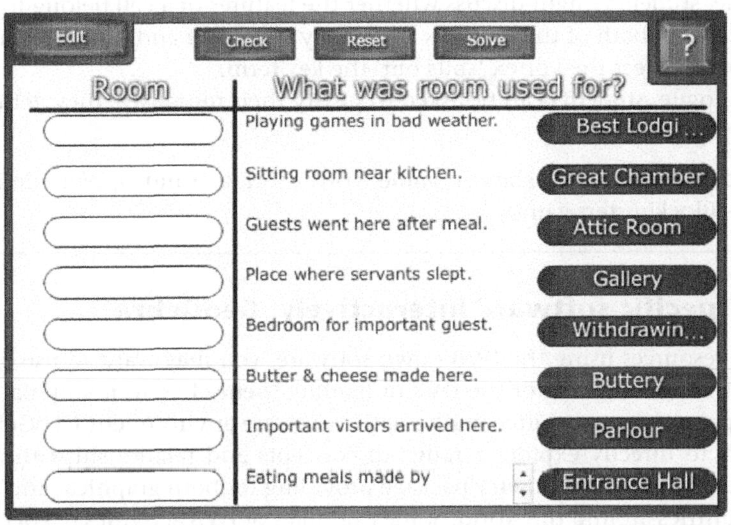

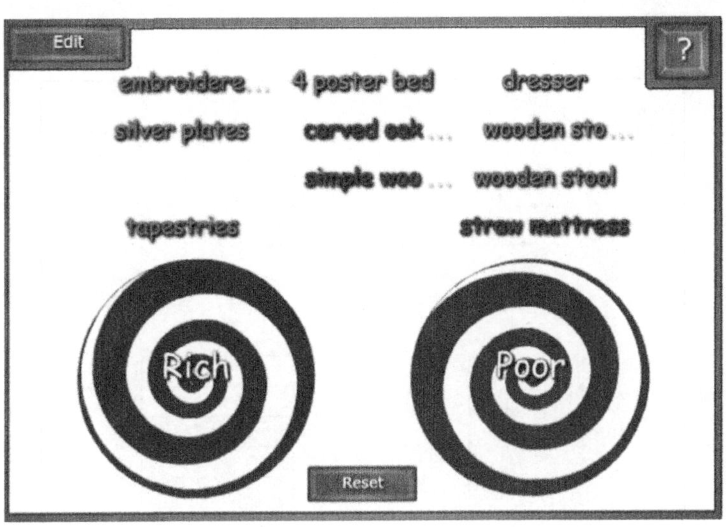

Sorting Activity - In this example pupils might discuss whether the features of a cell belong to a plant cell only or plant and animal cells. Pupils then come to the IWB and drag and drop the terms into the correct position. If they are incorrect the vortex 'spits out' the key term.

This can be found in Gallery, Lesson Activity Toolkit 1.0, Activities, Vortex sort.

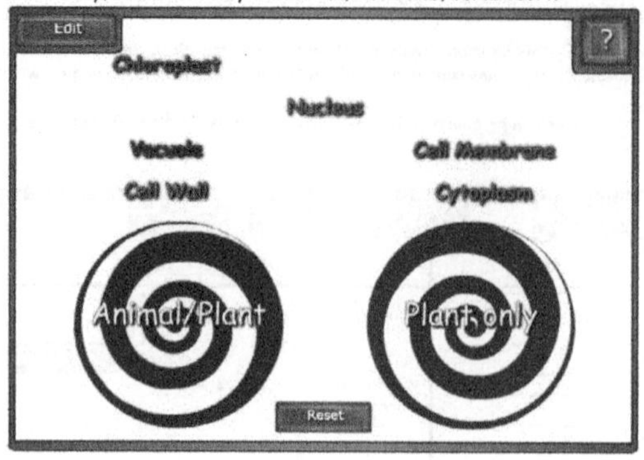

In the first example, students might discuss and match up the description to the key word. Similarly, in the second example, students demonstrate whether they know the names and uses of rooms in the house of a rich Tudor. Following discussion, definitions can then be added to/amended or deleted and reworded.

In the third example, students indicate what furniture the rich and poor Tudors might have had. In the final example, students might discuss whether the features of a cell belong to a plant cell only or plant and animal cells. In both of these vortex sorts, they then drag and drop the terms into the correct position. If they are incorrect the vortex 'spits out' the key term.

To promote dialogue, students can be asked to justify their responses; they get feedback both from the IWB and their peers/teacher.

See templates: Notebook ideas – Blockbusters game; Vortex sort (a, b and c); Word definitions (a, b and c); ActivInspire ideas – Blockbusters game

Using subject-specific software interactively: GeoGebra

As well as creating resources using the IWB's own software, you may want to use other software packages containing activities designed for the IWB or lending themselves to manipulation on a board. For example, the very powerful open source mathematics software environment GeoGebra (www.geogebra.org) allows learners to directly explore a range of concepts and relationships through manipulating objects on the screen. It is a free geometry package providing for both graphical and algebraic input and is used in many countries around the world. Some examples of IWB activities (GeoGebra format files are provided) are as follows.

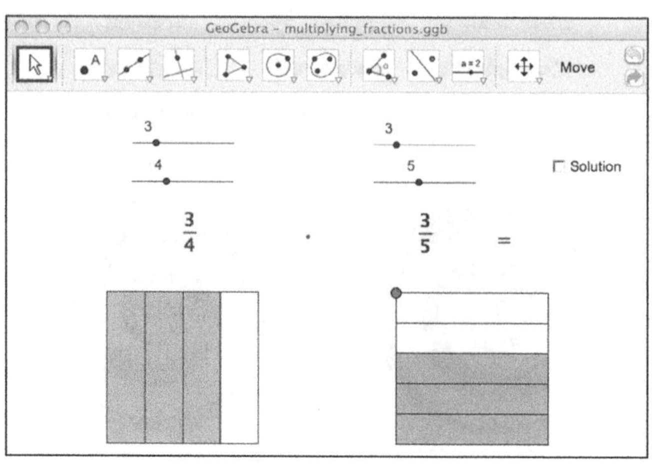

See Geogebra file: multiplying_fractions.ggb

You might ask questions like:

Change the fractions with the sliders and see what happens?
Move the blue point.
How many pink pieces does the square have? How can you get this number from the fractions?
How many purple pieces does the square have? How can you get this number from the fractions?

See Geogebra file: flower_symmetry.ggb

Is this flower symmetrical? Let's check by moving point D.
How many reflection lines does it have? Move points A and B. You can refresh the view if necessary (View: Refresh View or Ctrl+F).

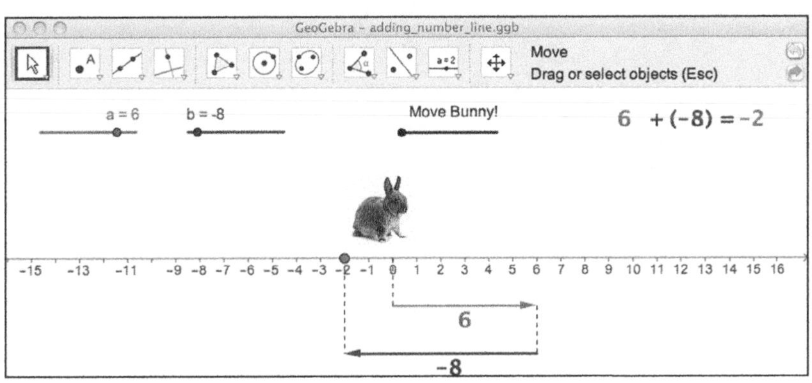

See Geogebra file: adding_number_line.ggb

Move Bunny! Change the values of a and b and move Bunny again!
In which case does Bunny make the turn?
When does Bunny look right/left?

Appendices

Downloadable versions of each Appendix can be found at http://tinyurl.com/OUPIWB.

Appendix A1 What do teachers use talk to do?

- Provide information.
- Check understanding.
- Maintain control.
- Link present activities to past experience.
- Set up future activities.
- Relate existing ideas to new educational frames of meaning.
- 'Model' educated ways of using language.

All of these functions of talk are important, but the last four can be thought of as being of a higher order than the first three. In particular, the last one links to the kinds of interactions that happen during dialogue. Thus, when language is used in what might be called an 'educated manner', you would expect to hear:

- Questions being used that support thinking
- Students being encouraged to elaborate or add detail
- Teachers and students challenging the thinking of members of the class
- Students being asked to give reasons, justify what they assert and speculate
- People negotiating their position and changing their mind.

Appendix A2 Dialogue table

Using the IWB to support the development of dialogue in the primary classroom		
In my classroom, we . . .	*You will see us . . .*	*So that we can . . .*
√ respect, trust and listen to each other √ take risks and experiment by trying out new teaching approaches √ encourage children to be responsible for their own learning √ use good subject knowledge and awareness of our children's needs to help us use children's contributions to advance the dialogue taking place √ support children in a range of ways to enable them to share their views and ideas √ value talk in our lessons and plan for it to take place √ are willing to sometimes change our minds √ continue a dialogue over time, from lesson to lesson √ use a wide range of IWB features and resources to stimulate, enhance and record aspects of our learning	√ sharing, discussing, commenting on and exploring our views and ideas √ asking each other questions √ showing that we consider other people's views √ sometimes trying to reach a shared understanding by building on what people say √ giving feedback and responding in a helpful way; being a 'critical friend' √ realizing what we need or would like to learn and doing something about it! √ using what we already know to help us √ reasoning and thinking aloud √ telling each other what we have learned when we have been thinking by ourselves √ using classroom resources, including the IWB, in different ways to help us in our learning √ saying why we agree or disagree with an idea	√ realize what we still need or want to learn and how we might like to do it √ extend and refine what we already know √ explain our reasoning clearly √ help each other to understand things in a new way √ come to agreement √ express a range of views

Appendix A3 Expanded dialogue table

Using the IWB to support the development of dialogue in the primary classroom		
In my classroom, we . . .	*You will see us . . .*	*So that we can . . .*
√ respect, trust and listen to each other ***school and class rules; pupil management; classroom working practice*** √ take risks and experiment by trying out new teaching approaches ***creative approaches; carefully chosen resources; groupings; pupil-led learning*** √ encourage children to be responsible for their own learning ***children involved in setting success criteria; children selecting ways of working*** √ use good subject knowledge and awareness of our children's needs to help us use children's contributions to advance the dialogue taking place ***teaching and planning founded on good subject knowledge; professional skill in adapting curriculum to meet particular needs of children*** √ support children in a range of ways to enable them to share their views and ideas ***use of additional adults; range of teaching and learning styles used; clear expectations and appropriate support/resources available so that all children can access the learning*** √ value talk in our lessons and plan for it to take place ***lessons are planned carefully to include opportunities to develop talk*** √ are willing to sometimes change our minds ***teacher and other adults model this; children encouraged to articulate it also*** √ continue a dialogue over time, from lesson to lesson ***planning takes account of this; teacher skill in maintaining continuity/recapping*** √ use a wide range of IWB features and resources to stimulate, enhance and record aspects of our learning ***IWB is used confidently in a range of ways, with teacher and children able to select and use features most appropriate to need***	√ sharing, discussing, commenting on and exploring our views and ideas √ asking each other questions √ showing that we consider other people's views √ sometimes trying to reach a shared understanding by building on what people say √ giving feedback and responding in a helpful way √ realizing what we need or would like to learn and doing something about it! √ using what we already know to help us √ reasoning and thinking aloud √ telling each other what we have learned when we have been thinking by ourselves √ using classroom resources, including the IWB, in different ways to help us in our learning √ saying why we agree or disagree with an idea	√ realize what we still need or want to learn and how we might like to do it ***children sometimes involved in setting agenda for future lessons; feedback from children on how they feel about their learning and what they still need; what questions has it raised?*** √ extend and refine what we already know ***new knowledge linked to existing knowledge; links between are clearly made*** √ explain our reasoning clearly ***improved speaking and listening skills; children are used to expectations of extended answers/explanations*** √ help each other to understand things in a new way ***children summarize learning; working co-operatively*** √ come to agreement √ express a range of views ***this is seen in the way in which children express their views and in how they receive and respond to the views of others***

Diane Rawlins, Arbury Primary School

Appendix A4 Edited extract from dialogue in Lloyd Brown's class around 'Is it possible for us to imagine the experience of trench warfare?'

Note: **Video 21** portrays this sequence in full.

Dillon: We don't actually know if that's true because it's a DVD. So because we weren't actually alive, some of that might be true, but we can't be sure. [. . .]

Ricky: It's like when you imagine winning the lottery . . . it wouldn't necessarily be like what you think.

Teacher (T): Very good. I think that's quite a nice analogy. I mean it's different, but it's almost beyond our experience. Alex?

Alex: I think there are probably bits we can imagine and bits we can't.

T: All right. Robert, can I take the point that you made? It links in with what Alex said. Listen to this. This is Robert's view.[1]

Robert: You can imagine what it would look like, but you can't imagine what it would feel like or how you would be feeling.

T: OK. What do you think about that Owen? [repeats Robert's comment] I quite like that.

Owen: Yes, because on the DVDs or on the films and the poems and stuff,[2] it explains and you can see what it looks like, in wasteland, and you're both in trenches, but you wouldn't know what it was like to go ages without food or water.

T: OK, go on Ricky.

Ricky: That's partially true, but you wouldn't know what it would be like to be shot by a bullet or be bombed or something. You wouldn't see what it looked like either.

T: Owen is nodding his head there in agreement with what you were saying . . . You know, this notion about it's something completely outside of our experience . . . I like that Robert and it wasn't what I'd thought of. I thought I was going to write something else on here. Yes 'what it looked like' [writing on board], not 'what it felt like'. You are then able to bring in all the things that Felix and Adill or Joe or whoever it was who came up with this idea [*indicates the first three categories listed on the IWB: see Fig. App. 4.1*]. So yes there are some things we can

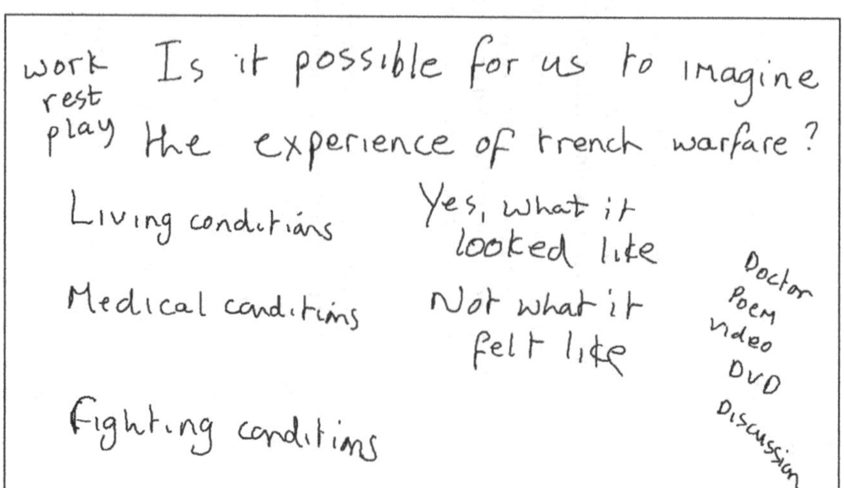

describe about it, but the actual feelings are rather difficult. Any other points to make here? Felix?

Felix: Well, about the feelings, every single person's experience with it would be different . . . Everybody's got different feelings towards the war . . . and you wouldn't know what anyone would have felt like, even if we were there, you would only know what you felt like.

T: Yes, can we ever achieve a common understanding of anything?

Notes

1. Lloyd deliberately brings in a significant comment he heard Robert make during pair work and then 'stored up'. He commonly used this strategy of bringing private interactions into the public arena, and constantly encouraged students to comment (respectfully) and build on others' viewpoints.
2. Owen's remark highlights the relevance of the vast range of resources previously interacted with on the IWB by the class.

Appendix A5 Creating a climate supportive for dialogue

For dialogue to thrive, the climate within the classroom needs to be a safe, stimulating and nurturing place where the teacher's intention is to make learning accessible to all children. Inclusive teaching approaches, based on a sound knowledge of pupils' strengths and needs, and which can be adapted between and within lessons, create the climate for dialogic teaching to take place. Some key aspects are:

Developing a learning community

- Create a safe environment within the classroom for risk-taking and working out or testing out ideas – give pupils experience in sharing ideas through gathering ideas from a number of children.
- Encourage peers to listen and speak to each other respectfully: 'Rewind and replay' gives them a second chance.
- Draw up Talk Rules with the class, making explicit your expectations relating to the dialogic approach and purpose of learning – through using dialogue.
- Acknowledge that not all learners will want to speak – offer other ways of sharing ideas and opinions, such as writing on Post-its and sorting/categorizing, shared writing on IWB pages, discussing in pairs/small groups.
- Exploit the flexibility/provisionality of the IWB and encourage students to generate and test provisional ideas – using flipchart pages to record ongoing discussions, returning to them and changing or adding to them.
- Inspire through enthusiasm – using creative ways to approach learning, trying out something different; explicitly showing interest in the learning, including pupils and teacher thinking of questions about the subject.
- Use supportive, open, friendly body language and encouraging facial expressions (smile!); these are especially important for pupils who may be wary of having their ideas rejected, or may find it difficult to absorb new information quickly and therefore need a more sensitive approach.
- Move away from the front of the classroom – circulate around students' tables or even sit at the back of his classroom while students share their ideas at the board.

Scaffolding[1] learning within the community

- Motivate and support individuals, groups or whole class – verbally (explaining, pre-teaching of vocabulary or key concepts, finding a 'way in' to a lesson which is engaging), visually (using artefacts, images on IWB) or through other media (music, video clips – IWB can enable all children to see and experience these well).
- Set appropriate level of challenge and constantly re-adjust – check previous learning experiences, to avoid 'we've already done this in Year 4'; use knowledge of pupils' skills and abilities to plan sufficient challenge (broadening experiences as well as extending).
- Recognize effort and progress – use focused praise related to dialogue and learning, e.g. 'That question you asked was great – I hadn't thought of that . . .', 'Our groups worked well today because you were listening carefully to each other's ideas . . .'; this makes progress explicit to pupils and creates a purposeful feel within the class.

Note

1. Scaffolding refers to a teacher providing individualized support to facilitate a learner's development. It is assistance that helps the learner progress further than they could have done alone.

Appendix A6 Teacher strategies for supporting dialogue with the IWB

This appendix includes a wide range of strategies and ideas that can be effective in promoting and developing dialogic teaching and learning in the classroom. There are areas that overlap, and the list is, of course, not exhaustive – we would be pleased to hear other suggestions and practical ideas that colleagues may have!

Developing pupil–pupil dialogue

- Encourage pupil–pupil talk – explicitly identify opportunities within lessons to get children talking in pairs and groups; you can ask them to evaluate their experience and feed this back into the class talk rules/class ground rules for talk; use talk partners to help children get used to learning through talking and sharing their ideas.
- Get pupils to monitor talk – this can be an interesting thing to do, as it enables children to recognize different aspects of dialogue (you could give them a simple checklist to look out for, e.g. agreeing, asking another person a question, disagreeing, changing your mind); we often ask children to report on what their group has been talking about – why not get them to report on how they are talking about it?
- Convey the significance of communication skills – explicitly stating why it is important to listen, comment, question, etc.
- Encourage and model productive dialogue: the impact of the teacher in developing this area is significant, especially when working on higher-order skills. Teachers can focus specifically on supporting pupils with:
  - justifying – drawing out reasons, asking for evidence
  - developing reasoning and application skills (e.g. interpreting visual images relevant to the lesson)
  - constructing arguments (e.g. by using role play or a storyline)
  - positioning – helping pupils to decide where they are with their thinking on a particular issue
  - evaluating ideas/claims/arguments by considering evidence (fact/opinion)
  - posing counter-arguments – e.g. playing devil's advocate.
- Develop dialogue skills – make it easy for pupils to participate in dialogue by having available (up on display on the IWB or on cards available for children to access easily) possible sentence openers, e.g. 'I agree with X because . . .', 'Could you explain a bit more about . . .?'

Continuing the development of learning over time

- Make the purpose and the scope of learning clear to children – give them the 'big picture' (how does our learning fit in with our daily lives and with what we already know?); use mind maps on the IWB to indicate how learning is developing, supplement with key images and annotations to represent key concepts – you can return to this at the start of a lesson or use it in the plenary to get children thinking about next steps
- Use children's experiences in and out of school to help to establish the context (e.g. in a unit of work about personal safety, share ideas about potential problems and difficulties which they may have encountered)
- Use a sequence of resources to follow a line of inquiry
- Save and revisit resources/annotations to re-ignite understanding: as well as using a straightforward mind-mapping technique, possibly expand the reviewing of ongoing learning by using class wikis, learning platforms, class discussion forums/blogs; make content accessible to children so they can continue learning outside the classroom (you could hyperlink to prior work or resources to support this); also, use the particular facilities of the IWB to make this exciting

and motivating, e.g. using games to match pairs, create the 'square of truth', posing multiple choice questions, challenging children to create an argument using key vocabulary and images which have been used throughout the learning (there are lots of Flash games which can be easily adapted and used with IWBs).

Involving pupils in co-constructing knowledge

For many teachers, this is an area that becomes a real turning point in the development of dialogue in their classrooms; the IWB is especially helpful in facilitating this (ideas below are largely IWB-focused).

- Give status to children's contributions, particularly encouraging them to be original; as well as giving focused praise and acknowledgement, these practical strategies are useful:
  - ask children to annotate flipchart pages with words, phrases, ideas, drawings, diagrams
  - use images/objects on flipchart pages for children to move about, link, shrink, enlarge, etc., getting them thinking about how they are showing what they understand
  - display work (on IWB or in other forms) for other groups to see (e.g. on a learning wall display – flipchart pages can be printed off and enlarged); this is motivating, gives status to children's input and may also stimulate continued discussion
  - save and print annotated flipcharts to use as a resource for talk groups
  - ask children to look at work from other groups, question each other, compare with their own group's perspective – teacher can actively bring in discussion about whether seeing other groups' work actually made us change our minds or help us to learn something new
  - give children the chance to work at the IWB to manipulate/link/develop ideas, e.g. give individuals/pairs a flipchart page to work on (encourage them to use hyperlinks to previous files from work in class or to link to helpful websites)
  - give children a set of photocopied mini-images and ask them to use images, words and phrases/sentences to construct diagrams which represent the outcomes of the dialogue/learning which has been taking place (this does allow for assessment of the level of children's understanding and their ability to distil this into a written form; some children will find this very challenging, and will do better to have the chance to talk it through with an adult so that their meaning can be made clear)
  - ask groups to present ideas to class, talking through and explaining them; encourage peers to comment.

Helping children to learn that ideas often change as we learn

This section is also heavily dependent on the climate for learning which exists in the classroom, and is greatly influenced by the level of teacher skill in supporting children in this more challenging aspect of dialogue:

- Model open-mindedness and tolerance of uncertainty.
- Really listen to pupil responses to fully understand what they are trying to convey – and handle unusual/unanticipated ones supportively.
- Discuss examples of when we have changed our minds, therefore showing children this can be a good thing to do.
- Be a genuine learning partner alongside children – it is very powerful for children to see ongoing learning happening to someone they may assume already knows everything!
- Demonstrate good subject knowledge and understanding of continuity and progression leading to building of knowledge through a unit of work.
- Sometimes withhold evaluative comments and feedback to encourage children to become more experienced in saying what they really mean/feel/want to say.
- Resist the urge to repeat children's responses or reformulate them – this shows that we expect responses to be listened to the first time; alongside this, encourage children to question each other (you can model this, e.g. 'I'd like to ask you something else about what you just said . . .', 'Does anyone else have a point they would like to make after hearing what X said?').
- Draw children into the learning through mystery, suspense, an unusual angle or approach, including withholding learning objectives sometimes; this encourages interest and motivation, and can also help children to identify with the learning going on.

These last sections comprise aspects of practice that can be worked on specifically by the teacher, either to develop their own competence and understanding, or with the children to give them experience, build up their confidence and help them to engage with learning through dialogue.

Guiding lesson flow

- Make sure you plan for different kinds of dialogue to take place at different stages in your lessons; e.g. presentational talk during plenaries, discussions to explore ideas gathered from group work.
- Set up focused pair discussions and use of mini (non-digital) whiteboards to record outcomes in preparation for IWB activity (e.g. creating a storyboard)
- Plan to use the IWB in a range of ways, especially involving pupils directly, e.g.:
  - try not to always use the IWB to frame a lesson – use it flexibly as the learning dictates
  - relinquish teacher control of the IWB and give children experience in using it actively and developmentally during a lesson
  - use the IWB alongside other non-digital resources (books, artefacts, paper, ordinary whiteboard or chalkboard) in an integrated way, as a place to draw together and keep ideas which you can return to at a later stage.

Developing pupil questioning

We often work on our own questioning skills as teachers, but less so on helping pupils to develop higher order questioning skills. You could have short, focused sessions to give pupils experience of approaches such as speculation, analogy, problem-solving, debate, analysis, synthesis, evaluation and 'thinking outside the box'. There are many resources around which could be used (e.g. in the various 'thinking skills' programmes available), but the particular facilities of the IWB make it extremely valuable here, e.g. making it possible to use sound, video, images and text very easily to stimulate a focused session. You can back this up with example open questions, key vocabulary, etc., to support children in beginning to make contributions.

Encouraging evaluation and synthesis

- Make evaluation and synthesis explicit through the language you use with pupils to help them understand what it happening; guide discussion sometimes, or sustain it (asking strategic questions, encouraging children to ask each other questions), use neutral encouragement to extend an argument ('Tell me a bit more about this . . .', 'Go on . . .'). If you are able to draw on saved, collective IWB work, you can make the synthesis and links very clear.
- Plan for thinking and talking time in your lessons – and allow enough time for this (too often we expect children to do a lot of thinking and talking in too short a time, and when they are not able to get to the point we want them to reach, we tell them what we wanted them to find out!); be sensitive and adaptive to all aspects of what is going on in the lesson, and keep the focus on the pace of learning, not just the pace of the lesson.

Appendix A7 How can you engage all learners in activity at the IWB?

Students enjoy contributing their own ideas on the IWB. It is fairly easy to ask a number of students to contribute something each on the board, for example underlining/highlighting some text or labelling a picture. This can be done quickly and is thought-provoking for others in the lesson. Alternative views to the ones placed on the flipchart can be recorded on another flipchart page. Both can easily be referred to by flipping between the different pages.

The IWB can also be used to record ideas over a longer period of lesson time. All members of the class can then access that information to help them with an assignment. The information can be saved for use in subsequent lessons and can act as a developing record of the ideas of the students in the class.

There may be opportunities for other students to give input or feedback when one student is at the board, for instance to guide them. Keeping everyone attentive rather than just watching is important.

Use of the IWB by students may be ongoing through the lesson. As students work on individual assignments after whole-class discussion, they can return to the board to record ideas that may not have come up on flipchart pages for others to use. In this way, even when students are working individually, they can collaborate. And, of course, material can be easily saved for use in the next lesson. This involves giving students the confidence to be able to contribute things that might not have been considered earlier in the lesson and requires a strong sense of the importance of collaborative learning.

What about activity away from the board? How can you engage *all* students including those who don't get a chance to come up to the IWB in the lesson?

You can use individual, mini (wipe-clean) whiteboards in class. These are really useful in helping students brainstorm ideas and are excellent as 'jotters'. For instance, we've used them to record pairs' ideas for a video storyboard or to capture individuals' reactions to a DVD before class discussion. If you want to collect ideas fairly quickly on the IWB, advance note taking on the mini-whiteboard can help this process. They help students to see that thinking about a question can be provisional and this is something else that the IWB can advance very effectively.

Students can also join in with an activity at their seats, for example by matching terms and definitions/functions, then justifying their own arrangements to peers. (As suggested in Part B, Reader, Chapter 5, using mini-images matching what is on the board is one possibility here; students can stick them in their books and annotate them to create their own personal record of IWB activity.) One learner could then arrange the ideas on the IWB with others verifying the arrangement. Making predictions and generating theories could also engage a whole class in this way.

Lloyd Brown, Chesterton Community College, Cambridge

Appendix A8 How can you find out what students think?

Questionnaires are a very effective way of providing feedback. We have found that students are remarkably honest in what they say in a questionnaire and this is very helpful in analysing the student experience of lessons. If the evidence is collected as soon as possible after the lesson or sequence of lessons, students will comment in more depth and forget less!

Videoing responses is another way to collect data. Sometimes you can capture more from an interview or recording. Some people are happier to talk about their lessons or find it easier to do so than write about their experiences. Flip cameras are cheap, unobtrusive and very user friendly. They can be used by individual students to record their thoughts themselves.

If you have videoed part of a lesson, it might be useful to watch a section of it with some students. You could prompt them for comments and seeing the lesson again will jog the memory of some.

Another creative and effective way to gather student views is by training student interviewers to interview their classmates. Sometimes, youngsters will be more open in talking to their peers rather than to their teachers.

Our school will also be experimenting with a Student Voice area, where we will collect video data on lessons (and other aspects of school life, chosen by staff and students) from the student perspective. It will essentially be managed by students who have recently been trained at a partner school in Student Voice techniques.

Lloyd Brown, Chesterton Community College, Cambridge

Appendix A9 Teaching and Learning Policy guidance and proposed action plan

Issues to be considered by Senior Management Team (SMT)

1. Quick review of existing Teaching and Learning Policy.
2. How does dialogic teaching and the dialogue table in particular fit in with our approach to teaching and learning (or vice versa!)?
3. Benefits for children.
4. Introducing this to staff.
5. Monitoring and evaluating.

Work with staff (over a series of staff meetings/team meetings)

1. Recap on dialogic teaching – what exactly is it?
2. Dialogic teaching 'audit' – using first column of dialogue table – including discussion about evidence ('How do we know?').
3. Share qualities of dialogic teaching already evident in our teaching (SMT to be ready with positive examples from performance management observations, e.g. classroom displays, interactive teaching styles, comments boxes in classrooms.)
4. Introduce dialogue table as the new 'guidance' element of our Teaching and Learning Policy – stress that actually very little of this will be new (this should be reassuring in terms of workload!). Explain how the table will serve as a framework to help us evaluate and enrich our approach to teaching.
5. Review use of IWB in classrooms – share examples of flipcharts/other IWB resources and how we used them, plus how children responded (opportunities for people to have additional IWB input if they want to).
6. Team meetings: collect examples of learning styles/activities/approaches for the 'You will see us . . .' column of the table. Add these to the table to be used when planning.
7. Agree to try out something, e.g. use of images (link this to PSHCE/SEAL work and all classes use the same images) and feedback at staff meeting about how children in different year groups responded – differently or with some similarities?
8. Team meetings: review of different types of dialogue we use in class, or could use. Link this to our work on improving writing and boosting speaking and listening throughout the school.
9. Monitoring and evaluating: discuss how we could evaluate our use of dialogic teaching. Possibilities include:
   - peer observation (issues relating to release time)
   - as part of performance management observations (by Head or Team Leader); some subject co-ordinators might like to focus their monitoring of teaching and learning on the impact of dialogic teaching approaches/strategies
   - children's responses: development of a checklist.

Diane Rawlins, Arbury Primary School

Appendix B6.1 Group interaction at the IWB – light sources and reflectors

This excerpt shows three children from a Year 5 class (ages 9–10) engaged in dialogue about where to place a glow-worm in a categorization of objects as light sources or reflectors. The IWB environment has been structured by the teacher to provide open access to all of the pages the children have encountered during the work. In this way the page sorter can act as an assistive memory for the students, should they need it.

S1: Oh that one's hard.

S2: Because it's a glow worm, that bit glows. So it's the light source.

S1: Yeah. It's probably the light source.

S3: Shall we write?

S2: It could, actually it could be both.

S1: Because it, yeah it could be both, that's (inaudible).

S3: So let's just.

S2: Shall we ask Mr (inaudible).

S3: Shall we just put it in the middle?

S1: For now yeah. Why do we think that?

(Students write on the smart board)

S1: Both. Because probably the light um, the glow worm the light bit, is probably um boun – the light from it bounces onto the um, the glow worm or something. Leave it Kaileigh ok?

S3: Right so, so right.

Discussion about other objects on screen, then a return to:

S2: What are you doing?

(One student draws on the smart board 'this one was hard')

S1: So let's go from.

S2: (inaudible) . . . that bit glows but that bit is the reflector.

S1: Yeah. Half of it's a reflector, and half of it is like that. Shall we just put um notes on each one?

S3: So that bit's the light.

S1: Put an arrow. Light source.

S2: That's the light source. And then this (inaudible).

S3: No, no, no, no do it in a different colour.

S2: Alright do it in a different.

(Students take it in turns to draw and write on smart board)

S1: And then the other one is the reflector, or the bug is the reflector. Shall we write in each one like why do we think that or not?

S2: No because we already know why (inaudible).

S1: Ok then, that's ok with me.

Appendix B6.2 Group interaction at the IWB – food chains

This excerpt shows three children from a Year 5 class (ages 9–10) engaged in dialogue about which animals and plants can be placed together in a food chain. The IWB environment has been structured by the teacher to provide screen elements that move and others that don't, plus hyperlinks to information about each organism.

S2: What do you think would eat the tree?

S3: Um, maybe the caterpillar might eat the tree?

S2: Not eat the whole tree.

S1: Well eat the plants.

S3: Yeah it'll eat the leaves.

S1: Wait let's just think about this. Let's see, that could go in there, and um then that, but that could be.

S3: Maybe the Mayfly could eat the leaves off the?

S2: I don't think (inaudible).

S1: No, no, no actually. Put this in there.

(One student removes the oak tree and replaces it with the algae)

S2: Algae.

S1: Then Mayfly, oh no back. Then maybe that could go on there yeah?

S3: Yeah.

S2: Oh what about the frog?

S3: But the frog could eat the Mayfly.

S1: Yeah eat that, and then the. What could be, what could the frog eat?

S3: No what could eat the frog? Maybe the owl could eat the frog?

S1: No, no.

S2: If a hedgehog was on there, that.

S1: Maybe.

S2: Unless if we could take that off, and put um, and put. Oh I know caterpillar.

S1: Yeah but that, the caterpillar wouldn't really eat that.

S2: Oh yeah no.

S1: That's in the water. Well so, we, why do you think that that could eat that?

S3: Because, and it lives in a habitat near the water.

S1: OK.

S3: For the foods that it's got is that is the best one.

S1: I think that could eat that, the fly because um. Mayfly because um.

S2: Because frogs can eat fly, frogs can eat flies.

S1: Because they both have the same.

S3: Why don't we write our answers on the board?

S1: Well actually; no, no, no, no. What about if we put that there, that could.

(Students click and drag the suggested answers into the boxes on the IWB)

S1: That could be eaten like that.

S2: Oh yeah.

S1: Because they, they basically all have the same habitat and so do they. But the water spider can probably eat that, and then.

S3: Maybe we could swap it round.

S1: No that's.

S2: Why was the spider (inaudible)?

S1: So do you all agree with that?

S3: Do you agree with that yeah?

S2: Yeah.

Appendix B7.1 Resources for searching with the Internet[1]

Compiled by Simon Knight

Resources

Some key videos, lesson plans, and tools to teach search skills are highlighted in the full version of this document (http://tinyurl.com/search5). You could also explore www.scoop.it/edu-search which lists lots of search tools and activities related to education. Many of these are visual tools, which could be used collaboratively on the IWB – for example, www.instagrok.com creates a concept map based on search terms, which students can then explore to learn more about the topic visually.

What are you searching for?

Asking students to find factual information is easier to assess, but it may not be the most effective use of time. You may have used 'Bloom's taxonomy' before to help you think about question stems; this may also be a useful prompt for search tasks too – from fact finding, to researching a problem and trying to create a solution.

You might also like to think about encouraging dialogue in the classroom through:

- using different search engines (visual search engines, search engines *within* a site or even just finding information on a particular page, rather than across the whole Web)
- encouraging justification of answers and source evaluation
- two part questions; for example, 'a google a day' (http://agoogleaday.com/) uses puzzles such as 'How many stories (officially) is the structure located at 350 5th Avenue in New York City?, which first requires knowing that said building is the Empire State, and then accessing a reasonable source to obtain the number of floors in the building.

There are some tools which explicitly support collaborative search which might be particularly useful alongside the IWB, for example: www.zakta.com; www.so.cl; and http://search-party.appspot.com/ (specifically designed for education); all support the sharing of: search terms; 'good' results; and discussion around search activities. See www.scoop.it/edu-search for more.

Note

1. This appendix is a summary of a document (http://tinyurl.com/search5) written by Simon Knight on the use of search engine tasks in classrooms, under a Creative Commons Attribution-ShareAlike licence. You are free to share and modify the page with attribution to this Dialogue and IWB resource.